Golden America

A MEMOIR

BELLA T. ALTURA

Copyright © 2014 Bella Altura
All rights reserved
First Edition

PAGE PUBLISHING, INC.
New York, NY

First originally published by Page Publishing, Inc. 2014

ISBN 978-1-63417-104-5 (pbk)
ISBN 978-1-63417-105-2 (digital)

Printed in the United States of America

For David, because he asked, and Rebecca, because she cares too.
Dedicated to the memory of my beloved parents.

Thank you to the staff at Page Publishing and to Ms. Elise J. Marton for their kind professional help.

PROLOGUE

I had a short childhood, but it was a happy one. I was born in a small town in Germany at the wrong time in history, the beginning of the Nazi era. Still, I did have a few years of normalcy.

My parents were happy and loving. How would I describe my mother? My mother was short in stature and felt soft and warm when she held me in her arms. She had light brown hair, which she combed away from her face in big curls; and when I was small, I liked to entangle my fingers in the abundant wealth of fluffiness. Her most outstanding characteristic, the first thing one surely noticed, were her deep blue eyes; the one thing my father, sadly, never saw because he was totally color-blind, as I realized years later. What a pity only I could recognize that stunning characteristic in my mother. And yet I did not tell her, ever, how beautiful her eyes were, nor did I ever tell her how much I admired her and how infinitely much I loved her. My father was, of course, the most handsome man in the world, whom I loved above everything else. I told him so, perhaps not in so many words, but in so many ways: running into his arms when he came home every evening, asking to play with him, begging him to read me stories—all of which he did only too gladly—and walking with him on various outings with my hand firmly ensconced in his.

My father   My mother

My mom worked in my dad's furniture store, so she would leave me with a nanny. There was a series of them, and I remember not liking a few until we got Betty, who became my favorite. My mom was always busy somehow. When she was not at my father's store, she liked to cook, and she liked to embroider things that seemed to take forever to complete. I knew she had embroidered the mantles of the Torahs that were taken out from the ark at our synagogue on Saturdays and paraded around. I also knew that all the beautiful tablecloths we used on Saturdays and holidays were embroidered by her. Moreover, I was the proud owner of a white jacket with multicolored flowers fashioned by her. I was allowed to wear it only on special occasions.

Every Friday morning, my mom cooked and baked up a storm to prepare for Shabbat, and I liked to watch her. I was allowed to make my own little challah (braided bread used on Shabbat), which my mother would bake next to the two big ones she had prepared, after a lengthy mixing of flour and eggs and water and yeast, all bought in the grocery store the day before. The whole wide kitchen table would be taken up by the goings-on. She chopped fish with a big hatchet to make the gefilte fish (chopped fish balls), she boiled cows' feet after having them carefully cleaned to make *sulze* (jellied meat) with little pieces of vegetables and secret ingredients I never deciphered. She made delicious chicken soup with a whole chicken cut into pieces. She bought the chicken from the *schochet* (a Jewish slaughterer) and washed and salted and washed it again for prescribed times to make it quite kosher. The soup would simmer slowly, with my favorite little yellow eggs swimming around in it and carrots and a bone from a cow. It also had celery and onions, leek and parsley, and parsnip and dill, which she would add after washing them all with great concentration, frowning with the effort. She baked potato kugel (baked potato dish), grating the potatoes with so much energy that her fingers would be red and scraped. In the oven, she also baked cakes she had made from scratch. As I watched, she would knead and flatten the dough with a wooden rolling pin, then shape it into squares for some or round for others, cakes that tasted delicious and sweet, always decorated with almonds or streusels or chocolate designs. Some I liked better than others. She would let me lick the leftover dough, a great delight for me. She then set the table and usually added extra places for strangers my father might bring home. Then my mother would give me a coin to put in the blue-and-white box for charity and for Jerusalem. On the wall, we had a picture of Theodor Herzl, who, I was told, would make sure we had a country of our own again one day named Palestine, where the city of Jerusalem would be rebuilt.

On Fridays, my father would come home early and bathe and put on his best suit to go to synagogue. He would take me by the hand, walking proudly with me, and allow me to stay next to him in that beautiful temple—in the men's section, not in the balcony where the women sat on Shabbat morning. My father had a strong and loud voice, almost as strong as that of the cantor, Mr. Okunsky, who was a large heavyset man, an imposing figure dressed in his *kittel* (a white smock worn at prayer). I was always happy to be allowed to sit and stand next to my father, feeling special to be there, and enjoyed his singing and loved him for it. On the High Holidays, I had to stay upstairs with my mother, who mostly would pray quietly, sometimes with tears in her eyes. She usually wore a white fur shawl she had inherited from her mother that smelled funny from having been carefully packaged up with mothballs all year.

When we came home from the temple on Friday nights, my father and I, we often brought with us a stranger, someone who was in transit and had no place to go or was too poor to have a Shabbat meal. My mother would have lit candles in a simple brass candelabrum on Fridays, but for the Holidays, she used a very tall, highly decorated silver one. Before we ate, my father would bless me with his hand on my head and then sing the kiddush (a prayer of thanks) over the wine and challah plate, the bread hidden by the cover my mother had embroidered with colorful threads and intricate designs. After the meal, which took quite some time what with the schmoozing and the eating of so many courses, my father would sing *zmires* (songs of thanks) and then intone the prayer of thanks for the food that we had enjoyed. By the time it was done, I would be almost asleep, but both my parents would still tuck me into bed with a kiss.

My dolls and toys

In my father's store, I spent some of my happiest times in the town. I enjoyed watching him show off his furniture to a customer, talking about the unique design, tapping on it to demonstrate its sturdiness by the sound it made, and praising the different attributes of the wood. It got so I would imitate him, and that always made him laugh and made me ashamed somehow. But my very favorite times in the store were when my best girlfriend, Anneliese, would come to meet me there. She had long blonde tresses, and little curls formed on top of her head or escaped from her tightly wound braids. She was the daughter of our carpenter, and we played many happy hours together with the dolls we brought with us. We always agreed about everything we did; I loved her dearly, my blonde friend Anneliese, and she loved me too.

My friend Anneliese on her first day in school

My mother encouraged me to be friends with some of the girls we met at the temple who were daughters of my parents' friends, but I did not like any of them, particularly not the one she pushed on me most. She was not pretty and was cross-eyed to boot, and I just did not want to—no, could not—play with her. Cruel of me, I am sure, as I realized much later, but I guess that's how children are. I did like the adults, though, all my parents' acquaintances, particularly the ones who had stores on the same street as my father's establishment. There were the Wolkenfelds, who had a men's store in which I played by hiding and running between the suits hanging all in a row; this surely did not please the owners, but they would let me do it for a while, steadily watching while they talked with my father. There was the jewelry store next door, owned by the Ritters, in which I admired the diamonds and other fine stones, stroking them and rearranging them in the cases. From there I received a tiny diamond ring on my fourth birthday, presented with great fanfare as to how precious it was, which I keep among my favorite possessions to this day. I see them before me still, the Ritters, a great big round lady with a kindly face, and a very skinny gentleman with glasses on the tip of his nose.

On Sundays, when the weather was good, we would go on outings in my father's pride and joy, his funny-looking car. We would go to the woods nearby and have a picnic, or we would go far into the Rhineland to make sure that the statue of the little mermaid, Lorelei, was still there watching at the edge of the river on a great big stone. Sometimes we drove as far as Köln to admire the imposing cathedral. We were usually accompanied by family friends, and there would be much joking and talking while the ladies spread out a big, comfortable blanket replete with goodies like potato salad, eggs and cheese, pickles and bread and cakes for lunch.

In the wintertime, Sundays were no fun. It was my father's job to take me out to "play," but I was always cold and suffered from frostbites on my toes and fingers. I did not like to walk, let alone play, in the deep snow that seemed to be always present. In fact, I was mostly reluctant to move at all in the scratchy wool outfits my mother made me wear. Even my underthings were made out of that scratchy wool. And so I usually stood there like a statue until I started to cry, and my father would take me home.

My very best outdoor times were when we all went to Le Coq, at the seashore in Belgium, where we met my favorite relatives: Aunt Dora, Uncle Harry, my cousin Ida, and my very favorite cousin, Joe. I had a great time cavorting in the warm sunshine on the sand, wading in the little waves at the edge of the ocean, and playing and building sand castles with cousin Joe, who was a few years older than I but very willing to treat me as an equal. Sometimes Joe would fly a kite that I was allowed to hold for short moments, and sometimes we were sat on the backs of donkeys, which were covered with soft fur blankets, to ride around for a while and explore the beach. There was a lot of love and fun and warmth gathered at that seashore, which lasted and lingered in my memory.

Joe and me at the beach in Le Coq

Betty, my nanny, was warm and good to me, and I loved her for it—so much so that I sometimes felt I was betraying my mother with my affection for her. She took me for my first trip to the countryside where her parents owned a farm. This was a happy time too—I got to see an entirely new and fascinating world: live chickens, whose eggs I gathered in the mornings; a colorful, noisy rooster; a goat with a silky brown beard; and, wonder of wonders, a pair of soft and shiny kittens that I could pet and keep in my lap. Life had never been this good for me, and never would be as good again. I ran in the fields; picked flowers, green beans, and tomatoes from vines and apples from trees; and adopted Betty's parents as my grandparents with the promise that they would invite me again and again. My own grandparents lived far away, somewhere in Poland. My father's mother did come to see us once for just a few weeks, not nearly long enough to form any kind of a relationship with me.

My nanny Betty

Betty had a twenty-year-old brother, Walter, who visited us at our home occasionally. I fell in love with him at the age of four. He solemnly promised he would wait for me until I grew old enough to marry him. He worked in a steel factory, and as proof of his good intentions, he gave me a small, authentic, silver pocket knife, a replica of a real one, which I put in the bottom of a drawer, only to look at and touch secretly once in a while.

One summer when I was six, my parents had the brainstorm to send me away to a sleepaway camp to prepare me for school and make me more independent. This turned out to be far from beneficial. In fact, from what I can recall, it was a disaster. From that place I remember two things. I clearly remember being left alone in the mess hall after all the other children had finished eating and gone to activities, because I could not eat the cherry soup they served for the first course of the meal. I tried and tried, sitting there all alone in front of that plate of soup, but it made me gag and finally vomit. The other thing I remember was standing in a circle of my peers at playtime, having to guess which girl hid a ball behind her back while they all held their arms behind theirs. It was a total enigma to me. I had no clue. I could not have guessed if my life depended on it, and so I just stared and stared and felt overcome with misery. At night, I cried myself to sleep. Luckily, I was sent home—dismissed dishonorably but finally able to breathe again.

When I was still five, I was asked to be a flower girl at a wedding in the next town over together with another five-year-old named Margot, who was the daughter of friends of my parents, and who became my friend for life. There is a long story to this friendship, and I will tell it later on; suffice it to say now that at that wedding, we met for the first time. I immediately admired her blonde hair and how she stayed so calm and was able to keep a little crown held tightly on her head while I was uncomfortable and fidgety and could not keep my crown on my slippery hair, the bane of my young existence.

Perhaps that wedding was a foreboding of what was to come for all of us. Four weeks after the wedding, we heard that the bride had died of heart failure although the groom was a cardiologist—not a good sign for his professional savvy or a good omen for Margot and me.

Margot and me at the wedding

THE CLOUDS GATHER

In the meantime, I had made friends with a baby who lived with her parents in the apartment above ours. She delighted me with her smiles and the gurgles she produced when I talked to her. Very shortly thereafter, however, my family was told we could not stay in the building. We had to move, suddenly, to another part of town, far away, and that was sad for me as it prevented me from seeing that friendly baby whom I had cherished and looked forward to visiting each day.

Well, I still had my friend Anneliese, but one dark day, I was told that she could no longer play with me. In fact, our carpenter—her father, who had worked for us ever since my father opened the store, was taken ill; he was operated on and died on the table—the fate of an honest Christian who was ordered but refused to give up his job working for a Jew, as I was told years later.

When I was finally old enough to enter first grade, it was not a good experience. For one thing, children starting school were traditionally given a big cardboard cone replete with candies of all sorts to bring to class on the first day of school, but mine contained no candies. Also, in class, all the children were seated next to each other, but I was seated in the back all by myself. When I raised my hand to answer a question, I was never called on, and I was prohibited to speak to any of the other children. I was sad, but no one gave me any explanation for these strange rules, so I just attended school as it was, feeling increasingly isolated and stupid.

Our relatives from Belgium had, meanwhile, the good sense to immigrate to "golden America," as it was called in our household. With great effort, they managed to send us papers, and later ship tickets, to join them. My father, however, constantly repeated that nothing bad could happen to us since he was friendly with all the neighbors and had many good friends all over the town and its environs due to his outgoing and easy personality. Therefore, he did not see a reason to leave. I remained in the dark as to what was happening since my parents never discussed anything untoward or important in German but spoke with each other in Polish, a language I could not understand. Yet when the ship tickets came, I was overjoyed and jumped up and down on our big easy chair because I thought we would be going to golden America, where my favorite cousin Joe lived and my aunt and uncle and cousin Ida. Two days after that joyous day, it was decreed that there would be no more going to golden America because the quota for us, whatever that meant, was closed.

My mother, who was the smart one in the family, hearing many rumors that terrible things were happening to Jews in Germany, decided to go to Belgium the first week of November of 1938 to see if she could arrange for us to move there. She spoke not a word of French, but we had acquaintances there, so she went to explore through them.

KRISTALLNACHT

It was the ninth of November, and I was tucked in bed with my nanny sleeping nearby and my father asleep in his bedroom. In the middle of the night, a terrible noise woke us up from our deepest sleep. About forty SS men in their uniforms broke down the door to our apartment and started screaming, commanding us to get up and get dressed. Three stayed around us, and the rest started to break everything in sight, violently crashing things against the walls and to the floor. The three pushed us out onto the street and made us walk away from the house then started to beat my dad with all their might. I cried loudly and wanted to get between my father and the beaters, but Betty held me back. The SS men turned to me between blows and screeched, "Be quiet, you dirty Jew urchin, or we will beat you too!" Betty dragged me away and made me walk down the dark street, away from the beating, but I tried to resist and hold back. Suddenly my father's cries stopped; the SS men had finished the job and walked away, seemingly leaving him for dead. I pulled the nanny with me toward him.

My father lay on the ground covered with blood and did not move. I screamed and Betty shook him gently, and by a miracle, he was still alive but barely so. Betty sat him up while still holding me tightly, and then two policemen came out of nowhere and got my father to stand up against a wall by kicking him with their boots. They wanted to take him to the police station and told me to go with Betty, but I refused to go, so they took me too. My father and I were put into a prison cell while Betty was sent away for she was not Jewish. I cried all night, lying on an iron cot watching my father bleed and bleed and listening to his terrible croaking, broken-up breathing and gasping for air. I threw up numerous times, until I could not bring up anything more, and lay there on the cot next to him, watching him and crying because I could not help him.

That was the end of my childhood, at the ripe old age of two weeks after my seventh birthday. But we were the lucky ones, as it turned out.

The next morning, Betty came to pick me up. I did not want to go, but my father, with labored breaths, begged me to go. My nanny dragged me along like a rag doll for I had lost all will. Then strangely, between sobs, I found that I could not utter a single word. I had lost my ability to speak. Betty, not knowing what to do, took me to the house of her brother Walter. They put me to bed, and for the next few days, they begged and cajoled to try to make me talk, but I could not say a word. I was devastated, and I cried. After three days, my mother came back from Belgium and promised me she would get my dad back. Slowly, a word at a time, I regained my speech, but I remained filled with fright and confusion.

My mother's trip to Belgium at that particular time surely saved her life. Had she been there with us, she would have forced herself between the SS and my father to protect him and certainly would have been shot.

My mother was the strong one in the family. She collected me from Walter's house, and we took a train to Düsseldorf to try and get papers to free my father, who had been shipped to the concentration camp Dachau. It took weeks as she ran with me to various officials, but she was able to finally get visas that would allow us to leave Germany and go to Belgium immediately. After four weeks in the camp, my father was freed, and we left by train for Belgium. Before leaving, we went back to see our apartment. There was nothing left in that apartment but shards and broken pieces. Every one of my dolls and stuffed animals was cut to bits, and so was all the furniture in my father's store. Even my favorite doll, Sonia, which had been hidden in the top of a closet because I was allowed to play with her only on holidays, was sliced into pieces. My mother searched for and found her two candlesticks and the menorah underneath the rubble. They were bent all out of shape, but she wrapped them in a sheet and took them along on our trip.

    I did not know how my parents felt about the devastation of their belongings. I never asked them what was on their minds when seeing the broken furniture, shattered lamps, glasses and china all over the floors, the cuckoo clock smashed, and the colorful crystal stemware in bits and pieces; I just hung on to their arms and begged to leave, far away to where it would be safe, desperately clinging to my father, who had just come back.

    I remember clearly, after we were seated in the train on our way to Belgium, my father went out again to buy some sandwiches to take along, and I, stiff with fright, panicked that he would miss the train, held my breath until he came back, and I could hold on to him.

BELGIUM

I n Brussels, where we settled, we lived near friends of my parents, and I was enrolled in school not knowing a word of French, the language that was spoken there. I entered class and, without any extra instruction, learned the language simply by listening. Shortly after I began at that school, Margot, whom I had met at the wedding three years earlier, enrolled in the same school. Her family had moved near us. We hugged and became best friends, and we also became rivals over our scholastic abilities. At that school—where I was treated as a normal child just like all the others, unlike what had happened in Germany—I discovered that I was a fast learner and, in fact, could outdo all the other children, including Margot, in short order. I got the best grades in all the class exams in every subject. That was a boon for me for it gave me some strength and self-esteem. The knowledge that I could learn easily provided the only inner strength I had, for the trauma of Kristallnacht had weakened my spirit and destroyed my self-image. I was convinced that my physical attributes were wretched. I hated my hair and I hated my looks and I even hated my name.

I never found out what my father did in Brussels to keep food on our table for he was not allowed to work, but my mother kept a nice home and cooked and cleaned. I became more attached to my parents. Night after night, I would wake up from terrible nightmares and tremblingly wander to their bed and lie down between them, in need of soothing and comfort.

Between school, playing with Margot, doing homework together, and going on outings to explore the city with our parents, the time passed by pleasantly, and we tried to forget the painful past.

After about a year of relative calm, however, my parents told me we would have to move again because the Germans were coming to Belgium. We needed to escape so we wouldn't wind up in a concentration camp as had so many other Jews from Germany and Poland, where we had many relatives and friends. I barely had time to say good-bye to Margot and to my teacher, Mademoiselle Verholen, whose favorite student I had become and whom I loved dearly. She had invited me several times to her house to meet her mother and to treat me with cocoa and cake. The last time, she had given me a beautiful wooden treasure box, all shiny and decorated in different colors, which I have held on to throughout my lengthy travels.

FRANCE

We had to be taken by smugglers from Belgium to France in the middle of the night because we had no papers allowing us to go there. It was very scary to sneak over the border by foot, groping around in the darkest of night, holding on to a stranger. Once over the border, we proceeded to Nice by train and met up there with relatives of my mom's, the Kerns—a family of three grown brothers, one of whom was married and had a boy of six, and one grown sister who came with her fiancé. These relatives were wealthy French citizens, but that would not make up for the fact that they were Jewish; and so they had fled Paris, where the Germans were headed to. We all lived in one apartment, and my mom did the cooking and cleaning for everybody since they all were used to having servants and not familiar with that kind of work; to me it was a boon for I liked the meals she prepared and was proud of her. How she felt about this arrangement, I did not know. I made fast friends with the little boy, Leon, who was two years younger than me, and since we were not enrolled in school, I devised games to play with him, some that he liked and others that he quickly got tired of. Sometimes we went to the beach with an adult. There was no sand as I was used to on a beach, but, rather, rounded pebbles of different sizes and colors, which were very hard to walk or sit on. But we still had fun wading in the ocean, which was quite blue, and collecting some of the more colorful pebbles to take home. We also took excursions to the environs to see interesting villas of rich people. Some of these homes had elaborate outdoor statues, which Leon and I would climb. The weather was always sunny and warm, particularly pleasant for me.

Leon and me in Nice at a villa

It was not very long though, a few months at most, before we had to leave again because the Germans were advancing into the south of France, and so my parents and I parted from our relatives and proceeded north by train to Grenoble, situated in the mountains. Here I was enrolled in school—new teachers, new pupils, a new curriculum, but at least the same language—while my parents found a place to live, and my father got a job in a bomb factory learning to make bombs. I soon became a good student again, first in my class, and it was here that I was introduced to and fell in love with biology watching my teacher dissect a bull's eye. I could not get over how that eye, which was once able to see the world around it, was reduced to pieces I could hold and touch! I never got over the amazement and decided that biology and everything about it was for me. Nothing else in school had ever interested me so, although I liked reading stories or learning in general. This exceeded all else; it was something to explore, something to absorb, something worth all my attention.

As luck would have it, my mom had to go back to Belgium for a few days to pick up some money she had left there, and she decided to take me along. The thought of traveling anywhere without my father terrified me—that plus the fact that my mother could still not speak a word of French, and the fact that we would be going into territory occupied by the Germans. My mother assured me we would be safe because she had false papers stating that we were French citizens. Our official story was that I had to have my tonsils taken out by a doctor in Belgium, and if anybody at the border asked us anything, I was to say that she was a mute. For the whole time of that trip, I was in a terrible panic. The trip to Brussels proceeded without a hitch, and for the trip back, my mother enveloped my neck with a big fur shawl into which, I knew, she had sewn the money she had retrieved in Brussels under the lining. She made me rehearse the story of my operation over and over again while I, by now a proud student of biology at the age of nine, knew full well that anybody looking into my throat would see that my tonsils were quite sound and quite present. At the French border, sure enough, a policeman stopped us and asked us for our papers. While showing the papers and trembling and in a complete panic, I told the story of my mother being a mute and how I had just had an operation to take out my tonsils. Well, the man must have been one of the righteous ones because after deliberating with himself and mumbling under his breath, he finally let us proceed with our journey. We arrived safe and sound back in Grenoble, but my panic would not subside until weeks later, further weakening me and making me less able to cope with more trauma.

Things heated up as the Germans marched further into France. Some of the Frenchmen were said to have leaked names and places of Jews living in Grenoble to earn points with the Germans, so my father transferred us to a small village in the mountains, where we had an apartment consisting of a single room and a hot plate for cooking. My father would work in the factory all week, where he had a place to sleep, and come to visit us on Sundays.

My mother, who had ingrained in her the idea that cleanliness is next to godliness, was seen by the neighbors to clean the outside steps that led to our room, much to their amazement. They would watch her and shake their heads, and I would panic every time for fear they would denounce us to the police. I attended school in that little village too, but it was no challenge for me. The curriculum consisted of reading, writing, and arithmetic—no history, no geography, and certainly no biology as I was used to from my time at the school in Grenoble—and so I became bored and looked forward to going home each day.

It happened one day that a close relative of my mother's, Aunt Toni, and one of her sons, Freddie, who was two years older than I, joined us there in that little village. They had fled from Brussels where Aunt Toni's husband had been taken to a concentration camp, grabbed from the street while he was walking, and my aunt had no inkling where the rest of her children, two more boys and one girl, had run to. My mother tended to my aunt, who was desolate and inconsolable, while I suddenly had a friend to play with after a long hiatus.

Freddie was into nature. He showed me how to capture lizards running in the grass, how they would grow back their tails after we pulled them off in our eagerness to place them in our homemade cages, and how to use worms to fish with homemade reels in a river, a new world for me. We fished and brought the delicate harvests home to be fried by my mother. The time with Freddie was a rare reprieve for me from the unease and repressed worries I always felt, a time of relaxation and precious joy. But it soon ended when my aunt departed with my new friend for another area in France to search for the rest of her children.

As for my mother and me, we had to deal with some large rats that suddenly appeared in our room to take the place of our relatives.

We told my father we heard mice, but he knew better from the size of the calling cards that they left. He set some traps and told us to hang our food on pieces of rope outside over the windowsill to keep it from being devoured. We stayed in that village for several more months, but then it was time to move on as the Germans were coming closer.

SWITZERLAND

Our next trip would not be by train at all but by walking deep into the Alps, and it would take three days and three nights to reach Switzerland, a free and neutral country. We were going to be taken across the border by some professional smugglers again, and they demanded almost all the money my father possessed to get us across. My mother prepared sandwiches for us, and after a long and arduous walk in the night, the first lap of our ascent, we met other Jewish people in a dark house. To go to the bathroom, I had to go outside; and when I passed a door, I saw a face staring at me through a glass window. Terrified, I ran to my mother and cried bitterly, and she said to me, in her own misery and not knowing how to console me, "When will you ever become a mensch?" This sentence has remained in my mind forever; it reverberated in my head and settled in my soul. My mother did not mean to hurt me; she did not mean it as a reproach, but I took it as such.

We stayed in that house during the day, hidden and quiet. The next night, we continued our trek over the mountains. The road became more and more arduous; it was straight up in parts, so we had to climb our way onward in snow and slippery ice. Many times, I stopped to tell my father I could not go on any farther, but he cajoled me and pushed me ahead until the sun started to come out, and we stopped and covered up with blankets to stay there, hidden, through daylight. The third night, the hiking was downhill, but after some hours, we suddenly were stopped by French police. The children and their parents were told to huddle together, and those adults without children or whose children were sixteen or older were sent back, right into the arms of the Germans. We were lucky because I was nine and allowed to continue the journey. The group that was left had been thinned out from ten families to three.

We walked farther down the mountains and finally came to a village at daybreak. The smugglers suddenly disappeared, and we were left to our own devices, supposedly free from persecution for the first time in years. I took deep breaths and my fright seemed to lighten with each breath taken. We, the three families left, sat down in the nearest café and ordered some breakfast. I looked longingly at a sugar cube, a delicacy I had not seen since we had left Germany. I was about to enjoy that treasure when, from the corner of my eyes, I saw soldiers approaching. I quickly turned away in order to make them disappear, but this ruse did not work. We were caught totally off guard, seemingly in bigger trouble than ever after that long and exhausting journey to "freedom." I was pretty much at the end of my rope. The soldiers allowed us to eat our breakfast, which I no longer wanted, and then made us come with them to a guardhouse, and the adults were interrogated as to their origins, abilities to work, and ages. I sat like a sack of flour, in deep despair, not an ounce of strength left, and clung to my parents, holding on to their arms. We were finally put into trucks and shipped off up a mountain to an internment camp, but at least we were still together, my parents and I. We were assigned a cot each and given blankets and told to settle in among the many other Jewish families that were already there.

As it turned out, this camp was not too bad. It was nothing like the concentration camps in Germany and Poland that we had heard about with dread and horror and had desperately tried to escape.

My strength returned somewhat with the passage of time, and some order set in. I was eventually able to detach from my parents and join the children, who were taken to activities. We played ball and other games, and I met and found a friend my age, Hannelore, or Jeanette as she called herself in French, and we stayed together throughout the days we spent in that camp. My mother was made to do sewing, at which she was proficient, and my father worked in the office. To my great pride, thanks to his easy and outgoing personality, he was unanimously elected to be the chief and official spokesman for all the refugees in that camp.

I started to settle in, spending all my waking time with Jeanette and playing various games in a special room with other children. To my amazement, we even were told we could become scouts; but to get to that lofty position, you had to bring a safety pin to attach a blue ribbon to your left sleeve. There was the rub: my mom owned only one safety pin, and she was using it to close the top of her blouse as she was very demure. I nagged her and nagged her to please let me have that safety pin, and she finally gave in, and then I was a full-fledged scout. What pride and joy. This lasted exactly one day, for the next day we were all shipped away, my parents separately—the men with the men, the women with the women—to two other camps, and I to a foster family I knew nothing about. Punishment is swift. This was for all the nagging I had done. Anyway, that is how I explained this turn of events to myself even to this day.

My mother in an interment camp in Switzerland near Luzern

My father in the internment camp in Switzerland near Lugano

FOSTER HOME

I was taken to a foster home by a lady who happened to be the daughter of the family that took me in, and for the whole train ride that it took to get there, I cried for my parents, quietly but steadily. The elderly lady who greeted me at the door of a house, in a town called Baden, was kindly and tried her best to console me by showing me a room I would have all to myself with some games and books and a real bed. I cried myself to sleep that evening. The next morning, I was given a breakfast of Bircher muesli, a delicate mixture of cereal, cream, and fruit—a specialty of Switzerland that became my favorite food. It was then explained to me that I would go to school, which was conducted in German in that part of Switzerland, but that the spoken language everywhere in the region was "Schwitzerdutch" (Swiss German), a German dialect that was utterly incomprehensible to me. The next day, I was enrolled in school, and wonder of wonders, my friend Jeanette was in the same class, having been taken in by another family in that same town. We were both overjoyed at this good luck. We hugged each other and vowed to be friends forever. Although we both had missed school for quite some time, we soon caught up, but the gibberish of the spoken language, even though derived from German, took us a while to first comprehend and then speak. We became friendly rivals scholastically and both fell in love with the gentleman teacher.

At "home," I got to like my foster mother and father, the Guggenheims, and became part of the family. I really liked the food that was prepared by my foster mother, and she insisted on teaching me the intricacies of Chinese checkers, which we played daily, and at which I finally became a whiz under her tutelage. I enjoyed the visits of their grown son and his family, his two children were fluent in German and French at the tender ages of four and five. On Saturdays, it became tradition for me to visit an elderly aunt, Tante Theresli, who lived in what I regarded as a beautiful apartment with many precious knickknacks that she would tell me about. She gave me hot cocoa and cookies and told me innumerable stories about her life and that of my foster family, all of which I enjoyed. The time always passed pleasantly for me, and she seemed to enjoy fussing over me and having my company.

It was the law of the land that foster children had to have instruction in their religion, so once a week, I went to a Jewish teacher who taught me to read and write in Hebrew—a job my father had undertaken previously—and told me things about the holidays and prayers. My life took on a pleasant routine, and I felt warmth around me, though I missed my parents.

I wrote to my mother and father weekly, and they did the same to me. I eagerly awaited their long letters and kept them close to my heart at night. Every three months, I was allowed to travel on a train to my mother's camp where, for three days, I would have a wonderful time being embraced by the love of my mother; meeting and visiting her camp mates, who showered me with warmth; and eating food specially prepared for me by a Swiss lady living near the camp, whom my mother paid to do so. Unfortunately, the time always flew by too quickly, and my trip back to the Guggenheims was a nightmare of tears shed from beginning to end of the train ride.

During the summer vacation, my foster mother decided to have me stay with another family that had two children, one my age, a girl named Ruthli, and the other a bit younger. Ruthli was going to the same school as I, but she was enrolled in the technical part of it while I was in the arts and science curriculum, which would allow me to continue on to college while she could not. She would have to go to a technical school to learn a trade. This made no difference to me—I had made friends with her during the daily recess—but it must have been a sore point to her mother, who was less than friendly or warm to me. The husband was a colonel in the army; he had a severe manner and did not bother with me. The family had a maid who was kind, and to her I gravitated for comfort. Well, things did not work out too well for me that summer. Though I enjoyed the company of the girls and had fun with them, I constantly felt scrutinized by the mother. One night, Ruthli and I were roughhousing it having a pillow fight, and we ended up in her bed, laughing and tickling each other. At that moment, the mother came into the room and reprimanded me severely. The next day, I was sent back to my foster parents, concluding that I had done something terrible. I buried this experience deep into my subconscious.

After the end of the year at my foster home, my foster mother told me I would have to go to another family as she needed the room I was occupying for the fiancé of her daughter, who would be coming to visit her often. This put me in a new turmoil; I would be uprooted again. I would be missing the school, my best friend Jeanette, who was remaining there, and the whole equilibrium I had built for myself in that town. My friend Jeanette invited me to her foster parents' house to say good-bye, and as I was walking there, I saw a rosebush in bloom in a garden. I wondered to myself, with much inner pain, how it was possible—and how lucky people could be—to be able to stay in one place long enough to grow roses.

I was sent to Bremgarten all by myself, and as usual, I cried bitterly all through the train ride. In between the tears, I saw that my train was circling its way down into a valley along a wide river, the first notable sight I became aware of in that beautiful country of Switzerland. At the station, a gentle lady greeted me, told me I should call her Tante Lina, and walked me down the main street. It began at a large gate and was flanked by remnants of walls, which had enclosed the whole town in ancient times, she explained to me. The street, lined by narrow houses, made a sharp turn, and there at the turn was my new foster home, over a men's store owned by my new foster father. The house itself was also narrow with steep stairs rising to two floors occupied by the owners.

I was introduced to the daughter, Susie, who stayed in Zurich most of the time to go to school, and to two sons, Kurt and Werner, who also were usually in Zurich—one at the university and the other at a technical school where he was learning to eventually take over the business of his father. I became the occupant of a narrow room with two beds, one of which was usually empty except when Susie came home to visit. I was enrolled in school the following day, where I had to find new friends and learn new rules along with new subjects. At least the language was the same.

Soon, not even three weeks into my stay in my new foster home, my foster mother, to whom I had grown attached, noticed something wrong with my health. She took me to Zurich to visit a specialist, who told her after I had been subjected to a lengthy, unpleasant examination that I had tuberculosis in one kidney and would have to be operated on within the next few days to remove the one kidney that was infected. It was a new bombshell for me, and I was overcome with fear once again. Both my parents were allowed to come to Zurich to stay with me for three days, and then they had to leave me there to be shipped off to Davos, to a sanatorium. I was to stay in Davos until I was healed from the operation and cured of the TB. As I sobbed, I made my foster mother promise that she would take me back into her home after I was discharged. She did promise me that; then she took me by train high into the Alps, to Davos, and left me there.

Once again, it was a strange new world for me. There were children from about ten to eighteen years old, I being the youngest at the time, in rooms with two to four occupants each. A Catholic nurse and a layperson were in charge, and there were strict rules to be followed. We got up, ate healthy food, played and rested at prescribed times, and those who did not have to stay in bed all day got to walk outside in a group in good weather. We were seen by a doctor every three months and told each time how much longer we would have to remain there. The afternoon repose, which took place after lunch until four o'clock, was the hardest because you were not allowed to speak, read, play, or do anything but rest under a warm blanket on a large balcony open to the fresh air.

On a walk in Davos, holding on to Schmidtli

I wrote sad letters to my parents at first but soon became attached to the layperson in charge. Her name was Schmidt, but everyone called her Schmidtli. She was a sweet lady, lighthearted and fun to be with, and fond of me. She even allowed me to become a kind of favorite; I was so needy for a substitute mother. I also was friends with my first roommate, who was quite a bit older than I; she was seventeen years old to my eleven. Soon, however, I was transferred out of the room I had become accustomed to, and this turned out to be a regular event; as soon as I became friends with my new roommate, I would be transferred out to another room. This and the fact that my adopted "mother," Schmidtli, was suddenly let go from her job, made me reluctantly realize that anti-Semitism was alive and well in Switzerland too. I was the only Jew in this publicly supported establishment to which I had been assigned, and the Catholic nurse did not like my presence.

It was all done under the ruse of financial necessity or for the good of other patients. For me, I had to grin and bear it. But despite this nurse, I never forgot that it was the Swiss government that allowed me to get my physical health back, and I was grateful for that. I also prayed to be allowed to leave soon, back to my foster mother's home.

Whenever a patient of the sanatorium was free of TB and discharged, it was customary for all the remaining children to assemble on the balconies and say good-bye loudly and with gusto, waving anything that looked vaguely like a flag, such as an undershirt or a blouse. It was a festive occasion. We all looked forward with great eagerness to the day that it would happen to us. When it was finally time for me to go after a long nine months, Sister Maria arranged her final coup against the little Jew she had been obliged to tend to. Nobody was allowed to cheer me on from the balconies when it was my turn to leave; I waited and looked back numerous times, but there was nobody, not even one of my friends, present to wave me good-bye . It hurt me deeply, but the fact was that I was out of there and going back to a warm and friendly family.

I eagerly awaited the final leg of my ride, the slow descent of the train as it followed the turn of the river. Tante Lina picked me up from the station and hugged me warmly. Back at the house, she prepared my favorite Bircher muesli as a treat. I went to sleep in my longed-for private room and was ready the next morning to finally go back to school again.

School was easy for me. There was much to catch up on, which was a special joy for me. By then I'd had plenty of practice in catching up. I made friends with a Swiss girl, and we had fun walking to and from school together as she lived two houses from "mine." The trips to my mother's camp were resumed, but this time on my way back, I did not cry because there were rumors that the war was finally coming to an end; the Germans were being defeated. I truly loved the people who had taken me in for a second time as promised, which gave me a much-needed sense of worth that I had lost. But the prospect of living with my parents again had been a sweet and unbelievably strong yearning that finally was going to be fulfilled.

Tante Lina had made me aware of my religion again, teaching me that it was necessary to say grace after meals to give thanks for the food we received, and to keep the Sabbath holy. I also had been taught religion by several different teachers as prescribed by the Swiss government. Among the teachers I had, there was one very Orthodox lady who instilled in me the need to become Orthodox myself around the time of the liberation from the German persecutions.

PEACE AT LAST

My joy to be reunited with my parents would not be without pain. Shortly before my parents were freed from the internment camps, I was told that my mother had contracted cancer during the stay in the camp, had been operated on, and had recuperated in a hotel in St. Moritz working as a chambermaid. This was prescribed to give her arm exercise, to get it moving again after the operation. I don't know how she was able to stand all that; I could not comprehend her ability to cope. But at the time, I buried the terrible news deep in my subconscious, as I was wont to do, and made believe it did not exist. It was so very uncaring of me, and I learned to live with much guilt. I loved my mother with all my heart, as I loved my father, but I did not want my reunion with them to be spoiled.

We were reunited in the south of Switzerland, near my father's internment camp. At long last we were together again, but each of us had gone through so much! It was such a relief to be free, but there were feelings of worries and insecurities to be overcome that would probably remain with us for a long time. Still, it was heaven to me to be together with my beloved parents again and hope grew that things could be wonderful again. There were prospects for my father to do some work even though, officially, he was not allowed to do so, and we were not allowed to stay in this country indefinitely. We immediately reapplied to go to golden America. The quota had been lifted, and my aunt and uncle were eager to have us come. My joy to be with my parents was total but very selfish. I just thought of myself: I wanted to be living and learning and did not want to let anything interfere with that goal. I wanted to be free, and I wanted to be able to express my wishes and needs, something one can only do with one's parents.

Before leaving my foster parents, I promised to stay in touch with them always, and I knew that they really cared for me and were interested in hearing good things.

LUGANO

We settled in Lugano where the language spoken was Italian. As we planned to go to America soon, I did not want to be enrolled in school for a short time and have to learn a new language to boot, but rather save my energy to learn English, secretly trying to rush the time I could devote myself to learn the subject I was longing for. The sooner I learned English, the sooner I would be able to devote myself to study biology. But to school I had to go, to that old routine of sitting in a class where every word was incomprehensible to me. I balked at the thought, so my parents enrolled me in a Catholic school attended by a girl I had befriended in the building where we had rented a room. This friend was a true gem and a true friend, taught by the nuns and her mother to be charitable and giving and good to the core of her being. Edith, or Editta as she was called in Italian, spoke German too, and she taught me and helped me over the hurdles of the new school. Under her tutelage, I learned Italian in a short time, and I also learned Latin, as she sat with me evening after evening helping me do part of my homework, which consisted of translating *The Iliad* from Latin to Italian, a difficult and impossible job to do by myself.

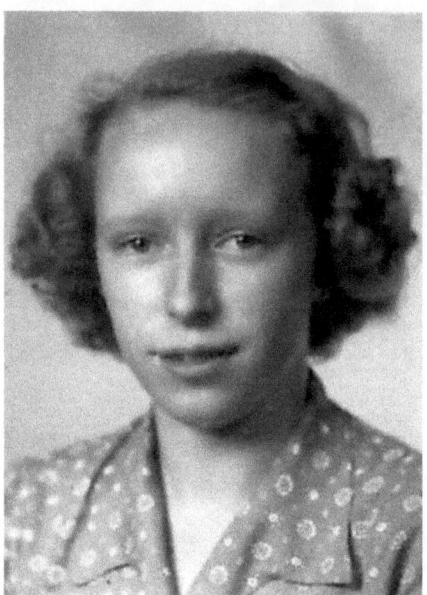

My friend Editta in Lugano

We also had great fun together on Sundays. I, in preparation to go to golden America, had been devouring books about that country, especially adventure books written by a German author, Karl May, who wrote detailed tales about Indians and how they lived before their land was invaded by the white man. Editta and I were fascinated with the adventures and built huts resembling what was described in the books, made Indian outfits with feathers and cardboard to imitate chieftain headgear, and carved long spears to go hunting into the make-believe woods. I had the time of my life, cramming a lost childhood and adolescence into a few weeks. Editta, too, was happy and enjoyed our playing together as she was an only child and usually spent her free time tending to her mother, who was a bedridden invalid. Life could not have been better.

GOLDEN AMERICA

Playing Indians with Editta in anticipation to coming to America.
To the left is a hut we built.

Another wonderful thing happened during our stay in Lugano. My cousin Joe, who had been living in America, had enlisted in the army and was now in Europe. He wrote to us that he would have time to visit us in Switzerland. What a joy this news was for all of us. First, he was my all-time favorite relative in the world, and I remembered him vividly from the good times we'd had at the seashore in Belgium, which seemed like ages ago. Well, he came and overwhelmed us all once again. He was handsome in his American uniform, and we could not stop admiring him and hugging him. He showered me with gifts like a fountain pen with the American army insignia, pins he took off his lapel, and American candy and chewing gum, a novelty for me. Joe was the old Joe I remembered. The few days he stayed with us were marred only by his relating to us terrible facts from having liberated a concentration camp, the atrocities of which we were hearing firsthand for the first time. We realized once more how lucky we were to have been spared unbelievable suffering by the good deed of the Swiss government in taking us in. Joe left with the promise of seeing us soon in

America for he was destined to be a civilian in a short time, and we would be joining him there soon.

We finally obtained the papers to embark to our final destination, golden America, after ten agony-filled years. I was sixteen by then and impatiently ready to start a new life free from worries and insecurities. I was very excited to have my parents with me in a free world; it would be ecstasy, yet leaving my friend Editta behind was nevertheless rather sad. So it was a bittersweet parting. We both shed some tears and hugged each other. I promised to write to her often, and she promised to write me back, a thing I knew I could count on.

We took a train and ferry to England to board a medium-size Cunard liner, *The Media*, to cross the Atlantic Ocean. In England, my mother wished to see a movie that was playing at the time, *Annie Get Your Gun*. However, because it was a Saturday, the Sabbath, and because I was anxious that something would go wrong with the trip, I didn't want to go, and I didn't want my parents to go either. Like the episode with the safety pin, this turned out to be another bit of guilt I had to internalize, deep into my subconscious, because that movie was the last bit of carefree fun my mother could have enjoyed.

AMERICA

The ship took six days to cross to America, and for all six days, I was seasick. That did not diminish my eagerness to arrive at my so-long-sought-after destination. Early on the seventh day, in what to me was a most majestic manner, the ship glided by the Statue of Liberty—the symbol we all had been waiting for through so many long and difficult years. We soon docked at the pier, and I ran to the deck. There I spotted my cousin Ida and I waved to her and strained to see my cousin Joe, whom I was most eager to see, and my aunt and uncle. Ida, however, was alone. After waving back to me, she left the spot where she was standing to look for my parents, and so I was left alone on the deck momentarily, nobody looking for me. As overwrought as I was, I found myself deeply disappointed for a moment. When we finally debarked, my aunt and uncle appeared and hugged and kissed me, and the joy returned. My parents were beside themselves with joy, and everyone talked at once, trying to impart the happiness they felt.

Processing our papers took some time, which gave me—characteristically—a great bit of anxiety (anyone in an official uniform was someone to be feared). We were then left to go with our newly recovered relatives. They took us to their home in Washington Heights, and we all had a wonderfully calming and restoring sleep.

Mother and me when things were good

Well, we had waited ten long years to come to this country. Nothing could have done justice to our expectations after so many hard years. I was only six years old when the thought of America first came to my attention, and not so much the picture but the feeling of it had remained with me as it had been then. I, of course, thought all would be as it had been before: we would have a nice home, my mother would return to being a housewife and helping my father, and my father would be able to earn a comfortable living while I went to school. As it turned out, I was quite unprepared for the realities as were, unfortunately, my parents. We were so happy to be free, together and free, but now it was time for my parents to settle into a new life, wounded though they were from all the trauma they had survived. My father was eager to get a job, any job, so long as he could start supporting us. My aunt and uncle, however, had not been financially successful in the approximately twelve years they had been in this country. This was totally unknown to my father, who was as naive now as he had been back in Germany when our troubles first began. Whatever my uncle counseled him, he took as gospel.

So after our first joy at being reunited with our relatives and our first happiness at having arrived in America had barely calmed down, my uncle took my father to his first step of becoming an American "millionaire," his words and his ideas. My uncle made him take every penny he had saved in Switzerland from his hard, honest work in the camps and then in Lugano, and use it to buy secondhand *schmattes* (cloth remnants), which he would be able to resell at enormous profit after they were sorted by color and type of material. My mother, who was still basking in the fact that she was close to her long-lost sister, was not told about this venture and so was not in on the decision to undertake it. To make a long sorry story short, after engaging my mother for a solid week to help sort the stuff into some semblance of order in a dusty, dirty room, my father had nothing to show for his money except an enormous amount of useless pieces of old cloth, which were not even salable below cost. Years later, I realized that my uncle had received a finder's fee from that transaction that had cost my father every hard-earned penny.

That happened two weeks after we arrived in America. I don't know how my mother and father felt about this turn of events—they never discussed things with me—but I tried to be oblivious to it as I enrolled in my last year of high school, some weeks after the school year had begun, knowing not a word of English. Well, I had been in that kind of predicament before, and with nothing but a strong will and the knowledge that I could do it, I managed to catch up. At the end of the school year, I was able to follow all my classes and do well. The only thing that gave me real trouble was current events, an integral part of history. It was very hard for me to comprehend the headlines of the newspaper articles we were assigned to read. The shorthand manner of titling these important and lengthy stories were beyond me then and are often still beyond me now.

My number-1 accomplishment that year was the biology Regents exam (an exam that would include questions from the whole subject matter learned by the class), which my teacher had doubts about my taking because it included botany, a subject I had not ever had before in any school. It had been taught to my class in the term before I showed up. The teacher was nice enough to lend me her botany book and told me to try and read it by myself and see what I could do. The result, I got a 100 on the biology Regents, which outdid all the other students. When word got out, I heard some strange teachers whispering about me as I went by. My own teacher hugged me as I returned the book to her and told me I surely had a great future ahead of me. Little did she know what troubles I would encounter before I had any future at all.

In the meantime, we had moved to an apartment in Morningside Heights, away from my aunt and uncle, and my mother opened a concession bakery all by herself with some borrowed money. She worked in that bakery seven days a week, selling baked goods that were delivered early in the morning. She was hampered by the fact that she spoke no English and so could not even socialize with the customers. My father tried to make a living working for someone else, going from store to store with some samples of silverware obtained from a cutlery retailer he had met at the temple.

I went to school on the subway, and I would stare at my peers in the train, or later at school, when they put on makeup—especially when they put on lipstick for what seemed to me like hours. I had been brought up to be modest and reserved, especially in my previous school where the prescribed dress code was a black smock with long sleeves. It had actually become my nature to be more severe in dress and appearance than we had to be back then, but this seemed to suit my personality. So, staring at the girls my age became a must-do as I tried to figure out what was possibly accomplished by their endless smearing up of their faces. I never made a friend at that high school, but I used my spare time to read any books I could get hold of by authors like Dostoyevsky, Tolstoy, Thomas Mann, and others. And I joined a Jewish

Orthodox group of girls, the Agudath Yisroel, on Saturdays where I found like-minded friends.

This kept me busy and also prevented me from helping my mother in any way. My poor mother, at one point, asked me to help with the dishes, but I told her I was too occupied with homework. She also asked me if it would be okay to take Mondays off and close the store on that day, but I told her she should close the store on Saturdays as that was the Sabbath, and no other day would do. She explained that the weekends were the best business days, and we needed the money, but I was relentless. My religiosity did not allow me to see the misery I created by my self-righteousness. How could I be so cruel? Now that it is years and years later, I cannot even start to comprehend my utter selfishness and lack of sympathy. My feeling of guilt is immeasurable, now and forever, and has been with me all these years. The truth was that my mother, too, would have liked to take off on Shabbat instead of any other day, but she was anxious to provide for us, and so she continued to work all week and did not allow herself another day of rest because of my unfortunate disapproval.

My mother continued to work seven days a week, no rest, no help, nothing to look forward to. My aunt never came to visit, nor did my cousins. They had changed in the years they had been in this country and seemed to be unsympathetic and hardened by their own insecure financial circumstances. I continued to go to school and do my homework when at home, join my friends on Saturdays, and spend the day reading on Sundays. I went on in this fashion even when my mother started to get headaches, which soon became constant.

On the day after my seventeenth birthday, my mother went to the hospital to be operated on; she had cancer of the brain. It was only a few months after we arrived in America. I had been totally in the dark, not having been told anything to spare me the worries, and not even thinking of anything other than my own world. I went to school as usual and then visited her afterward, but my mother never recognized me again or even knew that I was there. I went to visit her day after day, week after week, and every day expected her to get better, never capable to think otherwise. On Saturdays, one of my friends from the

Jewish group would walk with me the many blocks so I could see her. Two months after the operation, on one of my visits with my father at my side, we found that she was no longer in her bed. I imagined she had improved, so she had walked somewhere. A doctor came to take me aside and told me my mother had died.

I was numb and unresponsive. The next day at the funeral chapel, I fainted when they brought in my mother's coffin. My cousin Ida took me home. I could not go to the burial. I sat shivah (a Jewish custom of sitting on a low stool for one week except Saturdays) for one day. The next day was Saturday, and the following day, we sat shivah again. I don't remember that week.

My mother was an ideal mother, and she was called upon to prove it over and over again. She was the pillar of our family—her energy seemed boundless and her ability to cope unshakable. Wasn't it she who got my father out of the Dachau concentration camp when no one else could? She went from place to place, from authority to authority, with me, a frightened seven-year-old, in hand, and left no stone unturned until she was able to liberate him and bring him back to us. Wasn't it she who packed up what was left of our broken-down possessions and got us to Belgium with papers she somehow conjured up? Wasn't it she who managed to arrange places for us to stay and keep us together despite the fact that we had been totally displaced so many times, my father not allowed to work so many times? Wasn't it she who carried the heavy candlesticks wrapped in a sheet across the borders when we had to be smuggled, so we could always light candles on Shabbat. She finally got us safely to America after a long ten years of wandering. I never heard my mother complain, not once, during all those years; but often, she would remind us how lucky we were to be together and alive, the three of us. Yet she, like our forefather from long ago, when all was done and we were safe, was allowed only a short and distorted glimpse of the promised land.

LIFE WITHOUT MY MOTHER

My mother and father had been the backbone of my existence through all those miserable, difficult years. Now that my mother was gone, I felt that I had lost an integral part of myself, and a profound sadness set in. But I knew I had to manage two things: continue to go to school, and make a home for my father. Each day after school, I shopped and cooked and took care of the house, things that were totally new to me but I was determined to accomplish. I continued to observe the Sabbath and even invited acquaintances of my father for Friday-night meals, as I had remembered my mother had done back in Germany so he would have some company. My friends tried to cheer me up, but I stopped going to the Sabbath group, and I especially did not want to see my aunt and the rest of my relatives. Deep down inside, I resented my aunt being alive while my mother had passed away. I continued in this somber mood. I wrote to my friend Editta in Switzerland to tell her what had happened, and she wrote me back a long letter begging me to pull myself together. I never wrote her again. I wrote to my foster mother with similar results. I worked myself into a corner just doing what was required to survive.

One day out of the blue, my long-lost friend Margot came to America with her mother, aunt, and cousin. Both husbands had been taken off the street to concentration camp—Margot's father and her uncle—never to be heard from again while these four were hidden in an attic in Brussels all those years, tended to by some righteous neighbors. My father arranged for them to move to the house we were living in, and so I had one friend nearby whom I trusted and interacted with. The mothers learned to clean houses while Margot and her cousin, after mastering English in night school, worked in an office that required French and German translations.

Margot slowly coaxed me along to different places, like a Jewish refugee club or a walk through the city, but it was hard work for her. She soon became interested in boys, something that was foreign to me at that time. My goal was to go to college so I could study science and biology and, eventually, enter medical school, as that seemed the best place to learn what I was most interested in and give me the skills to use it in a profession. Therefore, any free time I had was devoted to studying. I applied to Hunter College, which was a prestigious girls' college in New York City where tuition was free. I was accepted and ventured on, continuing to cook and keep house for my father. He was working hard as a traveling salesman selling upholstery and drapery material, which took him rather far away sometimes. It was an odd occupation for him because of his color-blindness, but the samples he carried were clearly marked, and he sometimes asked me to verify the colors. This left me alone occasionally during the week, but since my friend and her family lived one floor below our apartment, I had their company when I needed it.

My studies were not quite as easy as before, my classmates having higher IQs than I was used to; but after a year, I got the hang of it and held my own. In school, I met a girl who had also been born in Germany, and we became friends very quickly. Helen had both her parents, having left Germany via England before all the trouble began. She took me under her wing, always present when I needed someone to talk to in school, and we visited each other's homes sometimes. She was fascinated with my kosher kitchen and made good-hearted fun of me when I scolded her for picking up a dairy utensil to eat meat and vice versa. I admired her well-kept, gracious home, complete with fancy German crystal and china I had not seen for ages. Two cousins lived with her. They were orphans, thanks to the concentration camps, and Helen's parents had brought them over from Europe. I could see that Helen had learned to have a good heart from her home environment.

Margot continued to encourage me to go out with her on Sundays, and one day, she took me to go dancing in the Jewish club we had joined. She met a boy she liked, and I was stuck with a young man who seemed to like me, but I thought he was boring and unattractive. That was my first encounter with boys, and I was not impressed. The whole arrangement of having to be chosen by someone did not appeal to me and went against my pride. The dating scene just remained foreign to me. Margot, in the meantime, brought her date home to meet the family and eventually became serious about him. That meant she would not have much time to spend with me. This hurt me, and I resented her future husband for it, but it liberated me from having to go to anymore dances.

My last year in college came along; I worked hard as usual and achieved Phi Beta Kappa status and was set to graduate with honors. In the meantime, I applied to a single medical school, Downstate in Brooklyn, a state-supported one since my father had no money available to pay tuition. The school put me on a waiting list but did not accept me outright.

Three weeks before my graduation, my father announced to me that he was going to get married. This surely was the worst timing he could have chosen. I was totally unprepared. I was unaware that he was seeing anybody, and I was dumbfounded at first then thrown into total chaos. I could not relate to his need of a mate, and replacing my beloved mother was heresy to me. I was twenty-one years old and had never had a date. I had continued to make a home for my father, cooking and cleaning and doing all the things necessary for the house while going to school. Here I was suddenly with no future: no place to go, no school to enter, no job, and definitely homeless. I suddenly felt totally unable to cope. I continued to go to class to the end of the school year, but it was agony for me. I knew my life, as I had known it, had ended. I could not see any future. I had nothing to turn to and felt devastated to the core.

After my graduation, which I did not attend, my depression continued. There was no way out of it, and my life became a nightmare. I sat around, could not eat or do anything at all. My father promised he would not get married if only I got better. This did not help. I did not know how to continue living.

My father took me to a doctor, but this did not help. In the meantime, since he had to go to work as a salesman on the road, he took me with him in the car. He also hired a lady to stay with me on some days and take care of the cooking. I sat around in despair and could only nourish myself with parts of peanut-butter sandwiches, prescribed by the doctor. I asked the lady to take care of my mother's clothes, which I had been unable to touch or remove from the closet for four years. I held on to some small items that she had been proud of and had the rest given to charity.

One day, while riding in the car with my father, I opened the door and jumped out of the moving car. I wanted to end the agony I was in. That was the only way I could cope with the pain. I fell to the road but was unhurt. I tried this again when we were going faster but only sustained some bruises I did not even feel. My father then placed me in a hospital.

I was given a bed next to some other girls around my age and was assigned a psychiatrist to see three times a week. She was tall and beautiful and had long, curly blonde hair. I admired her and tried to cooperate. At first it was useless because it was too difficult for me to talk. Gradually, very gradually, she helped me to communicate and tell her about my problems.

It was a long and difficult process exploring my inner feelings, talking about guilt and painful memories, but I trusted the doctor and even liked her. Whether I talked or just sat silent for the duration of the sessions was okay with her. She assigned me a social worker to whom

I could not relate at all. The social worker talked about things that did not interest me. I did participate in occupational therapy, making a wallet out of pieces of leather, etching a picture on a piece of metal. I was also given long hot baths to relax in. Eventually, I became friends with some of the other patients.

Slowly, I told the doctor things in my innermost being, which relieved me of some pain and made the guilt I felt toward my parents more bearable. But I was plagued by the fact that I had prevented my father from doing what he wanted to do—get married. So every time he was allowed to visit, I asked him to go ahead and get married. As for myself, after months and months of therapy, the doctor encouraged me, in time, to get a job and find a place to live, by myself or with a roommate.

Once in a while, there were dances in the recreation room of the hospital with young male patients, and I got to know and like one of the young men. He was good-looking, tall, blond, and not very sick, as far as I could tell. We did not talk about why we had been hospitalized but about our interests and hopes for the future. When we were allowed to go out, I went with him on my very first dates, and he managed to make the experience enjoyable. He took me to public clubs he knew where, for a few dollars, we could play Ping-Pong, which he taught me to play, and bridge, which I also learned from him. After a few dates, he was ready to ask me to become his girlfriend, but I said no to that as he was not Jewish, and I wanted to leave well enough alone. I had had a positive experience, and that was enough for me.

After a while, I was allowed to go out to look for a job, and I applied to a biochemistry laboratory where tests were done on blood and urine samples of very sick patients. Experience was not necessary as everything was being taught right there on the job, and this appealed to me. I got the job, and still living at the hospital, I started to work. It was immediately a good match. The work was not too difficult, but challenging enough to keep me interested and quite busy. There were eighteen other young people in the lab, and everyone was pleasant and fun to be with. There were two African-American secretaries whom I came to love because they were so good to me. They taught me how to enter the results I obtained from various analyses into the "big book" from which they then transferred the data on slips sent to the patients' charts. They always allowed me to interrupt them to enter my results anytime, a privilege only few of us were given. (The others had to wait until such time as the secretaries were done with what they were doing.) There was a small, skinny girl who had come from China recently, and she became my special friend. Susim had a great sense of humor, and her difficulty in speaking English—not being able to pronounce the letter *R* but using *L* instead—made for innumerable confusions and fun for us all. There was a diminutive Indian girl, Marjorie, who was solemn and very capable and tended to hang out with the two of us. There were young men we could always go to for help, when needed, to fix an instrument that did not want to work correctly, and there were other people who were smart and funny and always ready to play jokes on each other. Amazingly, for such a large crowd, there were no cliques; we seemed to be a group of one, all liking each other and all ready to help the one who needed it. Our supervisor, Gina, was a special person too, strict when it came to the work at hand, but fair and kind. The employees were a mixture of races and creeds, but everyone was a college graduate and most everyone had ambitions to further their education. Every week, we were assigned a different work partner, and I simply loved working with all of them. For the first time in a very long time, I actually experienced something akin to happiness again.

    I had become very friendly with one of the patients at my hospital, and when she was ready to leave the place, I was too. Pat asked me if I would like to become her roommate. That sounded ideal to me, and we found a small apartment consisting of one room plus a kitchen and a bath on the West Side of Manhattan. My father was taken aback when I did not return to his house, but I told him I would never do that again, and he could definitely get married.

A SECOND CHANCE

I was increasingly happy at my job and living with my roommate but continued to see my psychiatrist twice and then once a week, and if I ran into a problem, she would see me when she could manage, and thus help me over any difficulties I encountered. She was kind enough to charge me a minimal fee so I could afford the payments on my own, and I never had to ask my father for any financial help. My father did get married, and when he did, although I had repeatedly told him to go ahead with it, I was angry and did not talk to him for several weeks. I guess this was anger I had buried inside myself when the matter first came up, but I was too upset, confused, and desperate at the time to even be aware of it, among all the other emotions I felt. I let the anger peter out eventually and saw my father again, but only by himself. I never wanted to go near his wife.

With the encouragement of my doctor, after a year or so of working, I enrolled in night school to earn a master's degree in biology and rediscovered my love of studying, after all the agony and pain I had survived. It took a few years of night school, but I did earn my master's degree. I was so grateful to the school and to this country to be able to accomplish this feat at night while working full-time.

Meanwhile, at work, I had become a senior person, able to do all the tests that were run there. I had also acquired a sense of humor and a loud laugh that resonated all the way into the hallway. In fact, to my own amazement, I became the clown of the place, and my colleagues encouraged my antics so they could hear me laugh. I also worked nights once a week, and every sixth weekend from Friday evening until Monday morning, continuing on for the rest of the day on Monday with the day shift. This extra work was well paid, and I liked the responsibility of doing the work by myself. I thus had a full and satisfying job.

As time passed, new people were hired; one to replace a girl who got married, and another to replace a fellow who went back to school full-time for a higher degree. One of the new people who came on board was a tall, very thin young man with a rather narrow head, a perfectly straight nose—not at all what I was used to for a Jewish person (the ones I knew and was related to all had hook noses), extraordinarily long eyelashes, and a crew cut of black hair. He seemed to catch on very quickly to the tasks to be done, did his day's work in record time, and then delighted in spending his free time sitting on the desk of one of the secretaries, talking to her incessantly. One day, Willa, one of the secretaries, suggested that he take me out on a date, partly out of kindness to me, and partly so she wouldn't have to listen to his long discussions all the time. I was unaware of her promptings and did not pay any more attention to him than to any other coworker.

When it was time to share a task for a week with this young man, named Burt, I was amazed at his strange personality. Besides doing the assigned work very efficiently and incredibly quickly, he talked incessantly with me too, as he had done with the secretary. I found that he would pick a topic that piqued his interest and hold forth without stopping, regardless of the fact that I could not contribute a syllable to the conversation. The most amazing thing was that the talk was never boring or inane; by the end of the week, I had learned more from his "seminars" (as I secretly called his speeches) on many different topics than I had learned in all the years I had spent in this country. He spoke about the stock market, politics, the gene theory, DNA, RNA, the double helix of Watson—who had really stolen the idea from Rosalind Franklin and Erwin Chargaff, Darwin's discoveries in the Galapagos, and the delicacy of Chinese food in a certain restaurant on Long Island. By the end of each day of working with Burt, I was surprised at how much I had learned, but also at how little he minded or even noticed the fact that I was totally ignorant compared with him, could contribute nothing to the conversation, had a load of hang-ups, and was altogether a nonperson.

At the end of that fateful week, Burt asked me to go with him to try Chinese food, promising me he would order only the best. I was reluctant to accept, not only because I was a bore and had all sorts of difficulties I did not wish him to be burdened with for even one evening, but also because I had my doubts as to whether Chinese food was quite kosher. Well, just as he had convinced me during the workweek that he knew what he was talking about on every subject, he convinced me to go for Chinese food on Long Island. We went in his little green car, and that in itself was a memorable experience for the ride was very long, and every few miles, we had to stop to feed oil to the little green car's engine or else it would not putter any further. This did not bother Burt one bit, nor did it stop him from holding forth on the topic of his choice that evening: the intricacies of extracting DNA from leukemic cells of mice. He assured me that no one had attempted this as yet and that he would definitely be successful at comparing the base ratios of the DNA from those cells with cells from normal mice and use this as a basis for a master's thesis. When we finally arrived at the restaurant, I dutifully ate Chinese food for the first time and found it really tasted good, putting out of my mind the idea that it might not have been totally kosher. We returned to New York, puttering along in the green car as before with oil feedings and a new topic: the McCarthy years and the radical left.

The following week, I was scheduled to go on vacation and had made plans to go to the seashore all by myself to relax and catch up with some homework for night school, having enrolled again to continue my education. To make a long story short, as it was Sunday, I bought the *New York Times* and went to sit on the beach, which was strangely empty, to do the crossword puzzle—my favorite hobby. To my consternation, the magazine was missing from the paper, so no puzzle was available, and no sooner had I gotten over that disappointment than a policeman came over to tell me no one was allowed on the beach on Sundays in that town. I would have to pack up and go home. Embarrassed and very annoyed, I ventured into the first Chinese restaurant I could find to try to savor again that taste I had experienced with Burt two days before. Instead, I got deathly ill soon after and went back to my hotel, stretched out on the bed, and waited to die. This did not happen, but the next day, I checked out to return home and spend the rest of the week lazing around the apartment.

The following Monday, I reluctantly told Burt of my misadventure, and he triumphantly and in all seriousness assured me that I was destined to go out only with him. And so it was that, to begin with, we ate lunch together every day, going down to the cafeteria separately so as not to make it obvious to our coworkers. Soon Burt helped me at work, even if we were not assigned together, because he was always done with his tasks hours before everybody else—so much so that I suspected he mixed all the samples to be analyzed together and did just one analysis instead of several dozen. Instead, I found out that he brought an unwavering concentration, an economy of motion, and a clear method of operation to whatever he did, which allowed him to finish the work in record time.

Then he started to help me with my evening courses; calculus was Greek to me, but pass I did with his patient instruction. On my nights in the lab, he would stay with me just to keep me company and work on his master's thesis.

At the following Christmas party of the lab, the crew gave me a huge package. I unwrapped it, working through layer upon layer of tissue paper until, finally, I found a small snapshot of me looking up at Burt, taken by someone on the sly. Our carefully planned comings and goings had been discovered somehow.

Life became so different for me. I learned to take pleasure in things I had never enjoyed before, such as a stroll in Central Park, a ride in the country, going to the movies, visiting a museum, listening to music, always with Burt holding forth with some lecture of his choice. He never ran out of topics to talk about, and as time went by, I discovered his secret: he read everything he could get hold of on subjects that interested him, which were innumerable, and nothing seemed to escape his mind. He had pretty close to a photographic memory. In fact, nothing seemed to escape his notice except my so-obvious failings. To my astonishment, I slowly became comfortable in his company, and without being aware of the transition, Burt became indispensable to me.

Burt began asking to tie the knot between us. His patient entreaties were met with my steady refusals because I wanted to keep him from becoming burdened with the heavy emotional baggage I carried. After five years of this, I broke up with him to protect him from me. But after two unbearably miserable, excruciating days and sleepless nights, I could not rush to work fast enough to admit that if he still would have me, I would marry him; it seemed I could not do without him. And so we became engaged, and six months later were married.

LIFE IS GOOD

We had a small wedding between Christmas and New Year's, not to lose time from work or school, in a small temple in the presence of all our colleagues, my father and his wife, my cousin Ida—who was the maid of honor, and Burt's parents and two siblings. After a short ceremony (the rabbi did not know us, so was not able to say anything meaningful), there was a dinner with some background music; but to honor the memory of my mom, I did not want any dancing. We started our honeymoon, which Burt had arranged, the evening of the wedding, embarking to the Poconos. We said good-bye to friends and family and were taken to the train station by Ida. After a train ride of some hours, we were picked up by a van that would take us to the hotel; it was one o'clock in the morning, and we were the only passengers. The ride in the pitch-dark seemed to take forever. Just as we began thinking that surely we had been kidnapped, huddled together, holding on to each other for dear life, we did get to a cute cottage complete with a cozy living room with a fireplace, an old-fashioned canopy bed in the bedroom, and a Roman bath. Such luxury I had never encountered. Burt was unusually quiet, and I was suffused with a happiness I had never felt before.

The hotel was strictly for honeymoon couples. We participated in all the activities that were offered—we flew in a helicopter, went for hikes in the mountains, learned to shoot rifles, played Ping-Pong and volleyball, and enjoyed delicious food together with all the other couples. In the mornings, there was a news publication full of banter and fun and friendly gossip about the guests.

The days went by quickly, but we both enjoyed every minute, a preview of our life together. Back in New York, Burt moved into the tiny apartment I had shared with a roommate from the lab since my former roommate, Pat, had gotten married the year before, and I had relocated to a place near Memorial Hospital, our place of work. Wilma kindly moved out the day we were married. It was not much of an apartment, consisting of a kitchen and two closet-like areas on either side of the kitchen. We placed two cots in the "bedroom," which left no space to maneuver, so we had to climb out of bed over the foot of the cots. The "living room" just accommodated Burt's precious books—of which there were many, his oodles of records, and a marvelous record player that we placed on top of some bricks we had appropriated from the street. The kitchen contained a table and two chairs, and there was a bathroom off the entrance of our castle. On the sills outside our two windows—one in the "bedroom," the other in the "living room"—there lived several families of pigeons. When we opened the windows to get some air, the pigeons would march in and make themselves comfortable and proved difficult to shoo back out. So we decided it was better to forgo the fresh air to avoid the uninvited company. The place was totally primitive and spartan, but the monthly rent amounted to $37 for each of us, and work was just a few blocks away. We were happy, and I felt unbelievably blessed and rich.

Burt had continued his studies beyond his master's degree and got a stipend to study full-time in the pathology department of New York University, and I remained working in the lab, taking courses at night toward a PhD. Burt took over shopping for food because he claimed that my stinginess and counting of pennies would soon starve us. He also took over the cooking as his tastes ran toward simple, healthy meals that did not include heavy Jewish cooking. He did let me make salads and, occasionally, chicken soup. We sometimes had dinners out, which continued to feel like dates.

We worked hard and life was good. Burt's interest gravitated toward cardiovascular pathology and mine toward neurophysiology, but we kept each other informed of the details of both fields by discussing our day-to-day meanderings. As time went by, I too got a fellowship to study full-time for my last two years of degree work at Hunter College of the City University of New York, and I said goodbye with tears in my eyes to the friends I had made at my job and to the job itself, which had given me so much. Burt, by then, had gotten his PhD, and after many interviews and much cogitating, he took an assistant directorship of research in the department of anesthesiology at Albert Einstein College of Medicine under the tutelage of a senior anesthesiologist. He immediately was in charge of the research and was in total control of its direction. He was well paid for someone just out of graduate school, but he worked hard and long hours and seemed to be successful in everything he tried. We moved to a real apartment in Queens as the place we had occupied belonged to Memorial.

Meanwhile, I worked on frog nerves, studying the effect of calcium on peripheral nerves—which, at the time, was a hot and unexplored topic. I became good friends with another student, Judy, in the lab, and she helped me with some very finicky work, getting the membrane intimately attached to the nerve off without injuring the nerve itself, a task that was difficult for me. I was lucky my sponsor did not mind, but he knew that I did everything else with great diligence. When it was time to write up my thesis, Burt helped me put things into words with much patience and savvy; and even my sponsor helped, partly because he was ready to move to another position in another part of the country, and partly because he was excited about the outcome of my studies.

My friend Judy, who had been married for about a year, was eager to have a baby and promptly got pregnant. While she was working hard on my frog nerves, she urged me to do the same, considering that

I had been married five years by then. She talked at great length about its being the right thing to do, and as I was nearing the end of my studies, it also was the right time. I had not ever considered becoming a mother before, for the same reason I had hesitated so long to get married: I certainly would be an unfit mother with so much trauma I had survived, and I did not want to burden another being. I worried, too, that I could pass on weaknesses in my DNA, the stress I had endured having possibly caused lasting damage.

But Judy was persuasive, and Burt was thrilled with the idea, and shortly later, I too was having a baby. I had an easy pregnancy and never felt better all throughout, wondering how I could bottle the mixture of hormones making me so comfortable with myself. As long as I had a chocolate malted every day, everything was great, and I continued to work on my thesis to the very end. In fact, when Burt called my sponsor to tell him why I had not come to work the day of delivery, the sponsor said he had no doubt as to the reason. Feeling so good during my pregnancy made me think that I would breeze through the birth as well, but that was another matter altogether. I was quite unprepared for the pain, and for the first time, I was annoyed at Burt when, in the labor room, he proceeded to lecture the doctor at great length about the benefits of using one drug over another when anesthetizing rats for studies. I proceeded to yell loudly and repeatedly that I wanted him to be quiet, saying that I was the one needing the anesthesia, not the rats. This induced the resident who was assisting to tell me to shut up, which I took to be a great insult what with all the pain I was experiencing. It all seemed worth it in the end when a fat little baby with a head full of black hair appeared, seemingly perfect in all aspects. We had a beautiful daughter, whom we named Rachel after my mom. Burt was enchanted, and so was I.

When we took her home, we could not get over what a perfectly cute little thing she was. She was easy to hold because of her solid build. Every moment with her was sheer delight, and we both could not wait for her to wake up from her naps during the day so we could hold her and cuddle her and feed her and change her. The nights were a bit different though, we soon found out; she cried very loudly and persistently from about eleven o'clock to midnight. We were told by the pediatrician that she suffered from colic and would have to be walked for all that time. This task turned out to be somewhat hard for me, but Burt was delighted to keep her close to his chest where she held on for dear life, her little fingers intertwined with his abundant hair. She would stop crying with his walking back and forth and, after about an hour, would fall blissfully asleep. This went on for a full three months, after which it magically stopped, and she slept peacefully through the night. Burt did not know if he was happy about this turn of events; he kind of missed the lengthy togetherness when he had her all to himself. But I was grateful for the peace and quiet.

Rachel and her father

My thesis was all written up in the meantime, and the last step for me was to defend it in front of a committee including a dean of the university, my sponsor, another member of our faculty, and someone from another university, NYU, who was familiar with physiology and pharmacology in general. I was supposed to give a thirty-minute summary of my thesis by heart, and then answer any questions that would come up. I was extremely nervous about the procedure and spent the whole night before the event concentrating on memorizing my talk. Having not slept a wink, I went to a place unfamiliar to me for the ordeal. I was confident of only one thing: I could rattle off my thirty-minute speech flawlessly.

Well, the man from the other university was not familiar with the drill, and after the first sentence of my discourse, he asked me an esoteric question that threw me in a panic because all I wanted was to finish my talk and not forget any part of it, and think about questions later. After answering the question rather badly, I continued with my prepared speech, but the man asked me another question. This went on for the rest of the time, completely unhinging me. Fortunately, after I finally finished my talk, I was able to succinctly answer the questions that were asked by the other three members of the committee. When the ordeal was over, I was asked to leave the room and wait outside so the four could discuss my performance. Instead, seeing in my mind's eye my many years of hard work down the drain, I departed, running to catch the subway to go home and cry. I cried for a long while.

I found out later that my sponsor had spent a long time searching the streets looking for me so he could tell me I had passed. The dean, who knew that my thesis was a solid piece of work that I knew backward and forward, was satisfied and had had the final word. She also realized the problem that had occurred and instituted a new rule prohibiting any questions until the candidate completed his or her presentation. After a few rewrites of some parts of my thesis, which had been recommended by the committee, I was ready to graduate.

I took three months off to take care of our baby, although I had sworn that a baby would never keep me from going right back to work. The attachment one has for a child cannot possibly be imagined before the fact. After my cousin recommended a babysitter for our daughter, Burt invited me to work with him in his lab. Although my field was neurophysiology and his was cardiovascular physiology, I accepted his invitation provided that he would let me work on what interested me. I immediately started to study the effects of extracellular calcium on blood vessels, which was a new topic in the field and was of interest to Burt too. Well, it was not as simple as I had imagined. My work progressed, and things were fine at the lab, but I could not separate mentally from the daughter at home with the babysitter. I imagined all sorts of mishaps and even mishandlings and became increasingly anxious about her as time went by. After about six months, I could not endure the worries anymore, so I put my career on hold, took a leave of absence from work (lucky me, my boss did not mind), and stayed home to take care of my little one; home where I wanted to be, and where I was sure I belonged.

I never regretted for a minute having done that, even though I had worked so hard to have a career. My daughter came first, and the time I had with her was precious to me, and Burt agreed that I was doing the best for our family. I loved watching her grow. Every new thing she did was a monumental feat to me, and Burt loved to hear about her every adventure and progress. He could not wait to play with her on evenings and weekends. We took her everywhere we went; the thought of leaving her for an evening or afternoon never entered our minds. We even took her to the lab on weekends when Burt needed to be there. Her first words, after "dada" and "mama" and "shoe," were, to our astonishment, "epinephrine" and "crucible"—which she pronounced perfectly, pointing to a medicine cabinet on a visit for a checkup at her pediatrician.

When it was time for our daughter to enter preschool, I stood in the next room for the whole first day to make sure she would not miss me and cry; but she was fine, and after a couple of weeks, I started to consider going back to work. We began looking for a babysitter and found a lady both Burt and I liked, living in the building next to our apartment house. She had brought up two children of her own and had experience in taking care of others. She gladly took the job, and after a few days of observing her interaction with our daughter, I was ready to go back to the lab. True, several years had passed, but since Burt had kept me abreast of everything that was going on there, I had no trouble taking up where I had left off.

BACK TO WORK

The life of a scientist is quite different from that of most people with a nine-to-five job. Work for a scientist is really never done. You spend time in the lab doing experiments, which can often not be dropped simply because the time has arrived to go home. You go home when the work of that day is done—regardless of time. So some people work well into the night, or they install a cot and other necessities to stay overnight, going to sleep when the experiment can be left and continuing the next morning. Most importantly, there has to be time also to read scientific papers in order to stay abreast of the literature, to get ideas, and to avoid pursuing some path that has been worked out by someone else already. Therefore, when you leave the lab, there are still those pesky papers to be read, often in the subway and after dinner, once you've spent some quality time with the family. The weekends, of course, are ideal to do serious reading. Still, this task seems to be unending, and you often feel that you can never catch up; there is always one more journal to look over and one more paper to scan. Then there is the very difficult and sometimes useless task of writing a grant proposal for financial support of your experimental work. (I will describe this later.) But there are rewards too. When you are lucky enough to make a discovery, even a small one, you can relish the moment when you alone know something no one else is privy to and have come upon by diligent work, logic, and a bit of good luck. And there are the many wonderful places you see when going to scientific meetings to share your results with fellow scientists and hear others tell about theirs.

My first project was to study the effects of neurotransmitters (agents that affect nerve and muscle activity) normally present in the body on blood vessels of rats in the presence of various concentrations of calcium and normal concentrations of all the other ions usually found in circulating blood. The importance of these studies was to explore the effects calcium might have on the circulatory system since many doctors prescribe supplementation of calcium for bone health, especially to elderly women. I performed these experiments by studying little pieces of rat aorta stretched between two hooks in an aqueous bath at body temperature. Contractions or relaxations of the muscle were measured by a device that transferred the movements of the muscle to a pen producing lines on a piece of moving paper. Thus, I could accurately calculate even the smallest changes in the stretch of the muscle. The trick was to set up equal-size pieces of aorta in equal amounts of bathing solution and add accurately measured amounts of drugs or ions.

Before I began this study, I wanted to check the effects the neurotransmitters themselves had on the aortic muscle. I discovered, to my surprise, that depending on where I took the little piece of aorta from, in terms of its proximity to the heart, each piece acted differently. The farther away it was from the heart, the less the effect (contraction or relaxation) of the drug. This turned out to be true for all the neurotransmitters I tested. It was an unexpected result, so I repeated the experiments innumerable times because of my natural doubt before I reported it to Burt. Burt got all excited, which made me doubt myself some more, and we had our first real fight. He wanted to write up the results to be published in a scientific journal immediately, and I did not. I wanted to be cautious and wait, to repeat the work in other types of blood vessels. Burt, by then, had several technicians and postdoctoral fellows working under his direction, and so he was publishing papers and really did not need my little discovery right then. I eventually did write up a paper of this work, and it was accepted by a good journal.

Burt wrote many papers for publication—his mind was very prolific; he had more ideas to do experiments than hands to do them with—and he insisted I read each one to give my approval. I gladly did this, but it invariably resulted in a fight because although he trusted my judgment and said I was his most reliable critic, it was murder getting him to change one word of what he had written. This went on for each and every paper he passed by me, and it took me great fortitude and sweat to get the papers written so we were both satisfied. On occasion, I ran out of strength and gave in. He had a habit of sneaking in a sentence that necessitated a reference to some work he had previously published, even though it did not add anything to the paper at hand. Those were the sentences I fought the hardest to remove. Burt's excuse was that he wanted to quote his own work because no one else would, which was not really true. He soon became known as the prolific worker he was. Postdoctoral fellows from just about everywhere wanted to work in our lab, and he got invitations from all over the world to give seminars and talks.

We regularly went to scientific meetings in which his photographic memory came to the forefront and got people annoyed. He would get up to make comments such as "On page 665 of Circulation Research, 1973, volume 32, Dr. B. disagrees with your conclusion. Could you be mistaken?" This kind of thing did not make him too many friends. People usually could quote papers by author and journal, but pages, volume numbers, and dates no one remembered, and it gave the impression that Burt was rather arrogant.

I got along with everybody who worked in our lab over the years. Our technicians were my friends, and so were the MDs, postdoctoral fellows, and scientists who came from abroad and stayed with us for several years to advance their careers and learn techniques we had refined. They all became family. We had several people from Japan, several from China, and several from India. We had one scientist from

Brazil and one from Bulgaria, another from Chile, and so on. They all were a pleasure to have around, and they all worked hard to make their time count as much as possible. They published papers with us in good journals and, when back home, benefited from the experience by receiving promotions.

We often made parties and welcomed these scientists in our home. We stayed in touch with them all, and some invited us to their universities and their homes in those faraway places.

A STRANGER IN OUR MIDST

There was one exception, however, that we were unprepared for and cost us some pain. There was a young MD from Iran, an anesthesiologist trained in her country, who immigrated to the United States, was accepted in the anesthesiology department at Albert Einstein College of Medicine to do clinical work, and wanted to do some research in our lab for part of her training. We welcomed her in our lab, as we were accustomed in doing, but with time, things went bad; first, ever so subtly, then more obviously. The girl took it upon herself to organize our technicians to work fewer hours—come in late and leave early, and for some unknown reason, there suddenly was hostility toward me, something that had never happened before and had no apparent reason for my attitude and manner never changed. When it came time to write up a paper of her work, she took Burt aside and told him that she did not want to have my name associated with any of her papers since I had not done the work and did not belong as an author. Burt always put the name of the person who did the work first, an acknowledgment that this was the person responsible for the experiments, and put himself last as the person in whose lab the work was done and whose ideas and theories were propounded. Burt usually put my name in the middle if I had contributed ideas, had done related work, and had helped finalize the writing. The request she made was so out of order, and the atmosphere in our lab so strained, that Burt went over to ask the doctor in charge of her clinical work what he thought of her ability and work ethic. The man thanked him profusely for coming to talk to him and said that ever since she had come to work for him, his other clinicians were being organized to do less and less work, and everybody was at one another's throat. She was then asked to find another position, and when she finally left, our lab became the usual homey place we were accustomed to.

THE IVORY TOWER

In the meantime, to further study the effects of calcium on the cardiovascular system, I had turned to exploring the problem by using radioactive calcium-45, which allows for a very sensitive way of pinpointing the way calcium moved in and out of tissues. It was rather grueling work as one had to follow the ion by collecting samples of the bathing solution the pieces of blood vessel were hung up in, in little containers, every two minutes. One then had to add fresh solution. All this had to be done very accurately using a stopwatch and a pipette, and the solutions had to be kept at body temperature and prepared faultlessly. The calcium-45 in the collected liquid was later measured in a machine called a liquid scintillation counter. The experiments usually lasted for five hours uninterrupted. At the end, each piece of tissue was dried and carefully placed in a platinum crucible that had been washed in acid and rinsed in triple-distilled water to make sure there was no contamination with any foreign calcium. The tissue was ashed overnight in an oven at high temperature, and the resulting material dissolved and also measured in the liquid scintillation counter to account for the remaining radioactive calcium in the tissue. These experiments gave me results that were interesting and unexpected, so I repeated them over and over to make sure of their truth. When I calculated the results of all the experiments and showed them to Burt, he insisted they be written up and published at once. I, with my usual reluctance in believing my worth, held back.

It so happened that we were friends with another couple of scientists, a husband-and-wife team too, whom I admired greatly because of their high intellect and because the wife was able to work with an electron microscope, something I had tried but could not perfect. We socialized with them and, on one occasion, having lunch in their home, we discussed the results of my unpublished work. The husband smiled casually and told me that my conclusions were rather farfetched, and so I resisted Burt and did not let him publish all that lengthy and accurately done work. Not very long after that lunch, we found that our friends had published a paper about calcium in coronary blood vessels, which concluded what I had been blabbing about to them. Well, Burt to this day will not forgive me for not letting him publish that work promptly. In science, whoever publishes first gets the recognition! I did learn my lesson the hard way.

But any such annoyances were petty and unimportant and did not alter the fact that life was fun, and life was good for me always, from the moment I started to work.

Burt, around this time, was offered several prestigious positions in various parts of the country, mostly to become chairman of a physiology department or director of a group of scientists interested in what he was working on in faraway places like universities in California, Illinois, Michigan, and many others. But Rachel, our daughter, was enrolled in elementary school by then, and I was very reluctant to move her to another environment. Remembering from my past how difficult and painful it was to constantly move around from one place to another and from one school to another, I wanted to save her from such turmoil and begged Burt to stay in the city. As the positions he was offered were each more lucrative and prestigious than the previous, it was a real sacrifice for Burt not to accept any one of them, but he deferred to my wishes, and he took a position at another university in the city, the State University of New York Downstate Medical Center, with more lab space, a somewhat better salary, and a tenured full professor title at the age of thirty-five.

During the negotiations with the chairman of the new place, I was offered a position that would lead to tenure too if I agreed to teach medical students, but since I had never taught before, I could not see myself standing in front of a silent auditorium and was reluctant to do it. So I took an untenured position, and my salary would have to come from Burt's grants, of which he had several. Of course, that was a bad decision on my part. Several years later, I had to help out with the teaching due to a temporary lack of faculty. I found that I could teach and that teaching was the best way of understanding a subject. I could make things simple and clear to students once I made the effort of delving into the material thoroughly myself, by reading several textbooks on a particular subject, so as to see what was important to stress. It became a real benefit and satisfaction for me, and to my surprise, the students really liked me. Unfortunately, the same offer of a tenured position was, nonetheless, never repeated.

MORE IS NOT ALWAYS BETTER

Our department at the new university had only one liquid scintillation counter—located in our lab. I would have to share it with another professor who came on board from Mexico a few days after we did. This turned out to be a problem. I went to him first thing with the logical idea to alternate the days we used the instrument so we would not get into each other's way. He immediately answered that this would be impossible for him, and he ran to tell the chairman that he did not wish to be told by me, a lowly research associate, what to do. The chairman explained to me that, after all, this man was a full professor, and I would have to abide by his rules. Well, he used a radioactive material that gave off much stronger rays than my samples, and so he contaminated all 150 of my samples from an experiment I had run—a hard day's work down the drain because he did not want to alternate days with me. The next day, I repeated my work with a heavy heart and locked our lab to count my samples. When he found that the lab was locked, Professor Onesta ran up and down the corridor and screamed curses at me and told the chairman he would sue me for locking the lab. After this outrageous insult, which the chairman ignored, I decided to run my samples in the middle of the night (after my colleague had removed his) until I was done with that part of my project, and then never to use the liquid scintillation counter again, although this was wrong all the way around. I really had a hard time recovering from that experience. Since we had just started to work at that university, it resulted in my evading mixing with other colleagues. I stayed in our lab and only interacted with our group. Burt did not speak to the man again. Although I relinquished the instrument, and he took it into his lab, he gossiped to everyone he could about us.

He often socialized with the elite of the university, whom he wined and dined, being rather well-to-do and living in an area where most of the wealthier members of the university lived. Gossip was his bread and butter, as we found out later from one of his previous colleagues in Mexico. In fact, the faculty there was happy to see him leave because he had made trouble for some of his coworkers as he was now doing to us. The stories he told were made up in his head and all nonsense, but they made for good fun and entertainment for his guests at dinner parties. Burt could not possibly compete with that; he was incapable of making small talk and was not in with the higher-ups of the university. Gossiping or defending himself and me from idle talk was simply not in his DNA.

Professor Onesta was particularly friendly with one of the deans of the university in charge of graduate students. This dean's research specialty was the olfactory organ. She worked with snakes and seemed to have adopted their mannerisms; she hit swiftly and silently with deadly effect. We had taken on, against out better judgment (since this would take time away from our research and entailed added responsibility), a student who had completed his MD but wished to obtain a PhD in our lab. He worked hard, and when it was time to present some of his work to the faculty, I happened to meet the dean on the escalator and said hello to her. She almost bit my head off, saying in a very rough voice that she had no time to talk (I was not going to talk; I was just saying hello). This single encounter ensured that I would never speak to her again, and so our student was left with only Burt, who was constantly busy, to help him through. He prepared his written thesis, but the dean said it was much too long and had to be changed in its entirety. To make a long, sad story short, whatever the student did was always rejected; such was the power of the dean. In the middle of his effort to comply, the laws of procedure of obtaining a PhD were changed, and he had to start over by taking courses despite the fact that he already had his MD. Fed up, he gave up and moved on. All this happened because I had to share an instrument with Professor Onesta, and I still feel bad for the young man who was the ultimate victim.

But after some time elapsed, I did find colleagues I got to like and admire a lot. The first that comes to mind is Dr. Mario Vassalle, who came from Italy as a young man and still had a rather heavy Italian accent the students liked to complain about. He taught the physiology of the heart and was a great teacher, nonetheless, and very passionate when talking about the discoveries he had made pertaining to the heart. Whenever I had to help teach that particular area, I consulted with him; and over the years, we became friends. In his spare time, he wrote and published books on philosophy and composed beautiful poetry about nature, interwoven sometimes about some aspect of his work. They were written in Italian on one side of each page and translated into English on the opposite side. He had given me several of his books for a present, and I cherished them. There was one book called *Twilight*, another called *Dunes*, and a third called *Lost Emotions*, all of which I truly enjoyed reading and rereading. After a while, whenever he finished a new book, he asked me to make sure the translations were authentic and written in proper English. I loved doing this for him.

Another colleague I liked was Professor Kiyomi Koizumi, who had come from Japan, did research on the pituitary gland, and taught the endocrine part of physiology. She pushed me and encouraged me to do the teaching when it first came up that I was needed and, eventually, when she became interim-chairman, put me in charge of teaching physiology to physician's assistants, physical therapists, and diagnostic medical imaging students.

There was Dr. Alan Rudell, a computer expert and mathematics genius, way over my head, but he was friendly and we liked to talk politics. Then there were Lewis Gersten and Larry Eberle, technical assistants par excellence, who helped with teaching demonstrations and any other problems in the lab and were fun to kid around with.

And there were two people I admired and liked from afar. There was John Allen, a member of the research administration, who helped Burt with his financial problems and always gave him all his attention whenever there was some matter troubling him. I was in awe of him and very grateful that he had the patience to listen to Burt's complaints and help him manage his finances to do his research when the monies were starting to run out. He also occasionally looked over his written grant proposals and sometimes helped him even to write them.

Another person I admired from afar was Dr. Gerald Deas, whom Burt had befriended. Dr. Deas was the ideal doctor. He was on the faculty but still made house calls in the neighborhood and treated many patients for free. He often talked on a local radio station counseling listeners on ways to stay healthy. Dr. Deas made several videos for local TV with Burt. The two talked unrehearsed in a relaxed manner about the benefits of a healthy nutrition. The audience to which these talks were directed was known to eat poorly and missed the knowledge of how to stay healthy.

I never liked to intrude on Burt's friendships he made at work but respected his choices and was happy to hear him tell me about their interactions, just as he respected and let me have my friends.

We also befriended MDs from other departments, with whom we collaborated in clinical studies and chatted with about the work. They were from the department of obstetrics, anesthesiology, emergency medicine, neurology, and nephrology at Downstate. There were also a few researchers from other universities and even from abroad who came to bring me samples to analyze and stayed long enough to discuss details of results and, eventually, how to write up the papers. We all had an easy comradeship, glad to be working together.

DRUGS

At the same time as we had the unfortunate PhD student mentioned earlier, we had another student, a surgeon, who also wished to get a PhD with us. Burt was rather excited about him, because of his ability to handle intricate surgery, and put him on a project dear to his heart—something to do with shock and trauma. This surgeon was a hard worker and put in long hours with little rest; he had not yet completed his surgery residency, and so he had a limited time available in which to finish his work in our lab. It all worked out fine; Burt was happy about his results and his accuracy and diligence. There was one problem though, but I was too naive to recognize it at the time: he was into drugs. I found him one day with a rubber tube around his upper arm. Completely in the dark as to what that could mean, I joked that this would not be a good place to save rubber tubes for his circulation would be impaired. It never occurred to me what he was about to do. He laughed and said okay, that the upper arm was not where one saved rubber tubes, and took it off and put it in a drawer. I dismissed the matter completely. When he was done with his experiments, he went back to finish his surgery residency and promised he would work on writing the thesis in his spare time. One week after he left us, he was found dead of a drug overdose in the bathroom after performing a fourteen-hour operation. It was a terrible tragedy for all of us and for his parents and the university. We were shaken to the core and swore off having anything more to do with students. On reflection, it was my opinion that he loved doing research since he always seemed cheerful and happy in our lab and did not like to do surgery on patients. Maybe he had gone into it only because his father was a well-known surgeon. He also had many personal problems, which surfaced after he was gone. He actually had left a letter explaining some of his problems, in the drawer we had assigned to him in our lab. But knowing all these troubling matters did not make it any better for us. We never could publish the data he had worked so hard on; the whole thing was too painful to touch.

Be that as it may, we had to pull ourselves together and continue to work. I took on and devoted myself to a new project, and we were invited to many meetings in faraway places. We also managed to get one PhD student, Fann Wu, to finish her thesis and obtain her degree—despite the fact that we had sworn off students—after a new dean for graduate study was appointed.

A NEW PROJECT

Burt came to a discovery by sheer serendipity, as sometimes happens. He had made up a "normal Ringer solution" (a solution containing all the minerals found in blood) to bathe blood vessel tissues in, but had left out by mistake one of the many minerals normally present. As he studied the tissues in this faulty solution, he found that the tissue would give him abnormal results—that is, it would contract by itself without any hormones or drugs present. When he added contractile drugs, the tissue would react more forcefully, but when he tried relaxing drugs, the tissue would not relax. He was astute enough to realize what he had done wrong and was amazed at the results. Burt knew that magnesium, the particular mineral he had omitted from the bathing solution, had many effects on different tissues and enzymes, and so he asked me to repeat his preliminary "study," knowing full well that I would do it a thousand times before reporting on it. As it turned out, his chance discovery became our life's work; we studied the effect of the mineral in question in various tissues such as different blood vessels and the heart and found that it was an important mineral for health. Although epidemiological studies in the past (findings of people living in areas known to be low in this mineral in food and water) had pointed to this truth, no one had ever made an actual study of the mineral on cardiovascular tissues in physiology or studied the effect of its lack in pathology. We proceeded to do this, and it turned out to give us a wealth of information, enough to keep us happy for years.

We first performed many studies on animals. We found from these, for example, that a consistently low diet in magnesium produced elevated blood pressure in rats and atherosclerosis in rabbits. We then managed to reverse these effects by allowing the animals to have extra magnesium in their diet.

Burt then started to ask an acquaintance—and later, friend—of his from a biomedical company, Dr. Terry Shirey, and his colleagues to please prepare an electrode that would specifically measure ionized magnesium in human blood. The ionized form of any ion is interesting to study because it is the part of the element that is the active one. In other words, it is the part of any mineral that can affect health directly. The other part, the bound part of any element, is stuck and not usually active. There were plenty of electrodes on the market to measure ionized calcium, potassium, sodium, chloride, and others, but a magnesium-ion electrode had never been made because it was difficult on account of magnesium liking to bind to practically anything near it, and there were other minerals, especially calcium, which interfered with testing for it. After some months of work, Nova Biomedical from Waltham, Massachusetts, came up with an electrode and gave me the job to study it first, to see if it could be used effectively on blood of patients. I was thrilled with the task and spent some time to make sure the electrode gave accurate results, comparing it to standards prepared to contain specific amounts of ionized magnesium. It was a fun job as the electrode had peculiarities that had to be carefully taken into account or the results would be false. I spent a long time with this work in order to know when the electrode was okay to use and when it had to be thrown away. Nova Biomedical was very generous and not only gave me two instruments to use but as many electrodes of all kinds I wanted, and as many chemical reagents as necessary, for free.

After having been thoroughly acquainted with the new magnesium ion-selective electrode, we started to study human blood. First, I got a set of normal, healthy people to contribute a tube of their blood by begging, coaxing, bribing with some money, or simply asking them to contribute for the sake of science. This gave me a "normal range" that is a set of normal (healthy) values to which I could compare any diseased individual's to. I temporarily lost a lot of friends as they knew, once they came to visit, that I would come after them with a syringe and make sure they contributed a tube of blood. Then I started to use the electrode to study people who might give me interesting results, learned from the studies we did with animals. So, for example, I tested hypertensive patients and people who were known to have atherosclerosis. As the work became known, all sorts of doctors asked me to study some of their patients that they suspected would have abnormal amounts of magnesium in their blood.

We analyzed the blood of patients who suffered heart attacks and that of stroke patients, obtained from physicians who worked in the emergency room of our hospital, and found that if we got the blood early after the patient got sick, the ionized magnesium level in the blood was much decreased.

One of the most interesting studies were those of blood of patients from the University of Pittsburgh, who had obtained liver transplants and would have to take cyclosporine for the rest of their lives in order not to reject their new livers. While their livers seemed to work well, these patients would often suddenly die of massive heart attacks. I was the first one to report that patients taking cyclosporine had some of the least amounts of ionized magnesium in their blood. This was confirmed when someone brought me blood of patients with kidney transplants taking cyclosporine. These patients were then advised to take magnesium supplements, which prevented the nefarious outcomes and allowed many of them to live normal lives.

Another problem we explored were people with different types of headaches, whose samples of blood were supplied by a neurologist who headed a headache clinic in New York. We found that about 50 percent of patients with migraine had an abnormally low ionized magnesium level, and so did about half the patients who suffered from stress headaches. These particular patients were eventually infused with magnesium compounds intravenously, which subsequently reduced their headache attacks considerably.

A further interesting study we did was with pregnant women with the help of an obstetrician-gynecologist colleague (Dr. Sara Handwerker), and later with the chief of anesthesiology in our hospital. It had been known for a long time that some women suddenly develop high blood pressure during their pregnancy and often then lost their babies before birth or even died. Ever since the 1920s, it was suggested that infusions of magnesium sulfate would attenuate the high blood pressure and allow for a normal delivery in these patients. This treatment remained controversial for a long time. We tested such women for the ionized magnesium and found it to be very low at the time their blood pressure had increased. They were then given drips of magnesium sulfate intravenously and/or told to take oral supplements, which resulted in the reduction of their blood pressure and their babies being born healthy.

And so it went with many other studies, all of which I enjoyed doing and learning from.

We were privileged and grateful to see that other laboratories all over the world corroborated and continued our findings and have done so to this day. One of the clinicians interested in our studies was an emergency room physician, Dr. Mickey Schecter from Israel, who was able to put some of our results and those of others to the test in heart attack and stroke patients. He presented these in a meeting we attended, and we were very happy with his results.

One of the studies I directed was a study in rats fed only 10 percent of the usual amount of the mineral in food while administering it in various set amounts in their drinking water. This gave us a handle on the quantities of this mineral necessary for cardiovascular health, at least in rats.

We have been most gratified to hear that the prime minister of Israel, Benjamin Netanyahu, and his deputy health minister, Yaakov

Litzman, in May of 2012, allowed researchers to conduct a pilot study in an area of Israel that uses only desalinated water for drinking, by adding said mineral into the water supply. It was stated in the *Jerusalem Post* that there was no controversy from the science point of view. We feel particularly elated to have contributed something potentially significant to the health of the people of Israel.

In the meantime, Burt had turned his attention to a totally different problem. He had always been interested in the immune system of the body and how some people were resistant to stress and survived different diseases while others did badly or did not survive. He studied ways of stimulating the immune system of animals and found that he could increase it so much that animals would be resistant to diseases that they usually succumbed to. Burt also found that this resistance was due to a protein produced by the animals that had been stimulated, and that this protein could be injected into other animals to make them resistant too.

These studies were rather expensive to do, and so the money for them ran out before Burt could pinpoint the molecular structure of the particular protein that was so useful and beneficial. Someone else will certainly be able to take up were Burt left off and get the protein's formula worked out. That is what science is all about: the sharing of knowledge and ideas so that others can continue where one has left off.

TRAVELS

A part of being a scientist is to go to scientific meetings, and the more you become known, the more meetings you are invited to. These meetings give you a chance to present your work to as many other scientists as you can, not only to show what has been done in the field but to get input from them on how to continue, to see how your work fits in with other work in the field, and especially to learn what new studies have been done recently by others. In the end, it is a cross-fertilization of ideas and hypotheses that helps formulate new thoughts and new work. For us, it resulted in much travel to wonderful places, but it also meant we hardly ever took a real vacation. Instead, we would take an extra day here and there to get over jet lag and do some serious sightseeing in tandem with the conferences.

We went to Paris and Lisbon, Brussels and Budapest, Stockholm and Copenhagen, Rome and Florence, London and Athens, Crete and Jerusalem, Hawaii and different cities in Japan and China, and we never had to pay our way anywhere, the hosts covering all our expenses. We were treated as royalty and wined and dined and came home from each of these places with precious gifts given to us with warmth and chosen with special care. Burt usually gave a talk in each place, and I occasionally did too. There were other places we went to, like Leuven in Belgium, Zurich and Geneva in Switzerland, and chateaus in the Loire Valley in France. Each place had wonderful charm, and the hosts did their best to make us comfortable and happy. Burt also was in charge of several meetings in Los Angeles, San Diego, and Ventura, California. I cannot say enough about how kind and solicitous all our colleagues were. It had something to do with the fact that we were Americans first and scientists second. I must say I basked in the warmth of it all. I always came home feeling happy and so grateful to Burt and to this country, which gave us all these opportunities: the ability to work and to enjoy the fruits of our labor with a feeling of accomplishment we could be proud of.

An interesting corollary to our many trips was that we always got along famously with our European and Asian colleagues. Their first and foremost intent was to please us and everybody that was at the meetings. Our American colleagues were inherently different; they often had the need to show themselves as superior to others. The spirit of competition was ingrained and seemed to come unconsciously to the forefront. No harm was done, however. The matters simply resulted in vigorous discussions.

RACHEL

Since I was going to work every day and left Rachel with the babysitter, I had not become part of the social cliques of our apartment complex, and so Rachel had no way to be part of one of the children's playgroups either. She unfortunately had no friends in the neighborhood and could not make friends at school to play with either as there was no one to drive her anywhere. Finding friends to play with after school became a problem for her—and for me. I was always looking around, without success, to get her a friend to play with all during elementary school and even before. We did have friends (some of Burt's classmates) who had children that we visited with some Sundays and Rachel loved playing with, and we regularly went to the Macy's Thanksgiving parade every year (no matter how freezing it was) to meet with these friends and their children. But these occasions were far between as our friends all lived a distance from us, deep in Long Island, upstate New York, or New Jersey. Rachel also had fun and a loving relationship with Burt's parents and my father, but that too was an occasional thing. My dad called her his "sunshine," which she loved to hear, and Burt's father called her "boss-lady" (she was the only girl in his family), which she also enjoyed, and she usually had serious, lengthy private conversations with both her grandfathers and her grandmother when we were visiting with them.

During her last year in elementary school, she finally made a real friend, Tara, whose parents were helpful and gladly transported the kids back and forth, which greatly relieved me. I was so grateful to those parents, and we became friends too.

Rachel excelled in school and even skipped a grade before entering high school. There, she discovered a love for science, English, and learning in general, and found her way to the library to read on her own. She also appreciated art since we had taken her regularly to museums. Finally, I started to relax.

When Rachel was twelve years old, she wanted to enter an annual science competition. We suggested a simple project in which she would feed one group of mice with normal food and another with food deficient in magnesium. We provided the wherewithal, and she was very excited. After a few days, the mice with the mineral deficiency went into convulsions, an end result Rachel could easily observe. It was an expected finding but, of course, new for her. At the end, she amazed me by trying something I had told her would probably not work. But she insisted on dissolving some of the missing mineral from the food in water and injecting it into a mouse under the skin at the moment it went into convulsion. And lo and behold, the thing worked. The mouse stopped convulsing and was fine. Rachel constructed a nice poster describing her experiment, complete with pictures, results, and conclusions. She won first prize for her efforts.

The summer that she was fourteen, with the encouragement of one of her favorite teachers, Mort Rogen, we allowed her to go (with great trepidation on our part) to Michigan State University to work on a lab project that she could enter in the Westinghouse Science Talent Search, a prestigious national competition. She seemed to thrive there. She conducted a rather intricate project with the help of a very nice postdoctoral fellow in charge. She was successful in becoming a contestant and then a finalist, traveling to Washington to sightsee, speaking to various scientists and reporters, and even visiting the White House.

For college, Rachel applied and got accepted to Columbia, the University of Pennsylvania, Boston University, and Tufts, among others. Brandeis gave her a partial scholarship, and because it also was heavily Jewish, she chose to go there. She soon was working in a lab besides taking all the necessary courses to ready herself for medical school. For the first time, she made many friends, whom she kept up with all through the years, and she became rather religious. She graduated summa cum laude and went on to a prestigious medical school, Washington University in St. Louis, which accepted her as an MD-PhD student with all tuition paid by the school. She had already published a paper working in the biochemistry department at college and was coauthor of a paper derived from her Westinghouse project.

August 22, 1988

> We are accompanying Rachel to St. Louis, flying on TWA. But first, we have to get to the airport. She has an unbelievable amount of luggage—a guitar, valises, a trunk, framed prints packed in a blanket, a school bag, and she wants to take a carpet wrapped in plastic. Burt and I have a valise, a shopping bag full of newspapers, a flight bag, and Burt's well-traveled briefcase. It is impossible to get it all in the car. Burt's pessimism immediately triggers Rachel's belligerence. She launches into a tirade on the street by the parked car, loud enough for the whole neighborhood to hear. I am dreadfully embarrassed. After much yelling, the luggage goes into the trunk of the car and three boxes into the backseat. We all squeeze into the front seat, the guitar on our laps. The carpet stays home. It is a feat of engineering, brute force, and Rachel's temper. I tremble at the thought of the airplane flight, the trip from the airport in a rented car, and how we'll get it all into her assigned room up four flights of stairs. She has an iron will, and I am upset.

At the airport, everything makes it to the sidewalk while I sit as if anesthetized in the front seat. A check-in person takes pity on us and takes all the cargo material in hand while we are left with the paintings packed in the blanket, a flight bag, the newspapers, the guitar, and Burt's briefcase. We try to board, but the steward refuses the paintings and the guitar. Another scene develops, which further embarrasses me. A Hasid (a religious Jew) stands at the check-in line and watches with a sparkle in his eyes, his head downcast. Rachel is wearing a necklace with her name in Hebrew around her neck and a Brandeis sweatshirt with big Hebrew letters. Burt and the steward have a duel and a compromise is struck: the paintings go in with us (they are covered with glass), and the guitar will go in cargo. Rachel is pained at the thought of a broken guitar she has not touched in four years.

We board the plane, and I settle down between Rachel at the window and Burt across the aisle. I am soothed by the seating arrangement and proceed to look at some newspapers, magazines, and my favorite Sunday *Times* crossword puzzle. The flight is rather rocky, unusual for this time of the year, and Rachel gets anxious and leans on me. She accuses me of causing her to be afraid of flying because I never let her go on the big rides in Coney Island. I ignore the complaint and snuggle into my seat. The kosher snack we ordered helps sate our hunger. When we arrive, after much anxiety on Rachel's part, a sweet porter comes to our rescue. He takes the carry-on luggage from us and helps remove all the rest from the carousel, places the whole mess on a cart, and tells Burt where to bring the rented car so he can meet us there. Burt rents a Lincoln Town Car, a most gorgeous, brand-new specimen. The porter engineers it all into the car, and when we mention the four flights of stairs, he jokes that he will accompany us there to help us out. Burt gives him a tip to match the Lincoln, and we are somewhat relieved.

We find the dormitory after some wrong turns; asking directions is out of the question for Burt. Rachel takes possession of her room while we park nearby, and she comes downstairs, dejected. "The room is ugly as sin," she announces. "I hate it." We tell her to get a cart of some kind, and she returns with a hand truck that accommodates only one box. We climb up with one item each, and I discover that the room is quite nice—roomy, well lit, with a window all across its width and adequately furnished with a bed, a chair, a desk, a dresser, a closet, and built-in shelves for books. It even has a sink. I think the room is terrific. Rachel calls it a jail. I can't believe how spoiled she is. We carry the boxes and all the rest upstairs, one item at a time, and leave Rachel to fix up what she can while we check into a hotel.

When we pick her up for dinner, she has completely unpacked, stored her boxes in a storage room, hung up a beautiful Van Gogh poster on one wall and a Renoir on another. A Japanese silk cloth with delicately designed women is placed on her trunk to serve as a night table. Books are shelved; a stuffed Snoopy, a panda, and a white seal sit against the headboard; a little blue bucket in the shape of a heart rests next to the sink; and a blue-and-ecru mug with her college emblem carries her toothbrush. The room has been transformed into a peaceful place. She is somewhat pleased, and we go off to dine in an anchored boat-restaurant on the Mississippi. We enjoy a sumptuous meal complete with delicious Missouri champagne to celebrate a job well done. Though the place is mobbed, we are seated immediately, a pleasant change from the snooty New York restaurants whose maître d's would have laughed at us for asking for a table without a reservation.

When we return to the dormitory, we decide to explore and find a lovely reading room with high windows, a gym in which a volleyball game is in progress, an impressive interdenominational chapel, two TV rooms, and best of all, a corridor that leads directly to a marvelous library—a heaven at Rachel's fingertips: computers for student use, stacks and stacks of books and journals. Burt goes to the Science Citation Index to discover who has quoted us lately, and Rachel tries to find a paper she wrote last year. I caress the journals all in a row, bound, containing much work, much wisdom, and a little trash, which has to be weeded out. We leave Rachel after she meets a girl she recognizes from college, and they start talking. We return to the hotel, happy.

August 23

I did my job raising Rachel. My efforts and worries brought her this far, and the rest is up to her. She is in this great place; what she does with it is her business. I cannot teach her anymore or even advise her; she rejects everything. There is a breach between us. That's part of growing up, I tell myself. The umbilical cord has been severed for good (for her good, I hope).

I wonder what the world will be like for me without her, whom I have carried in the palms of my hands for twenty years. I tried to envelop her and protect her with all my ability and all my being, with all my heart. The effort was always first in my mind. I can identify with all those works of art, *Mother and Child*. There seemed to be nothing else that mattered as much all those years from the moment I held her in my arms, a chubby little being vaguely resembling my dad, vaguely resembling my husband (depending on which picture you looked at), but unique—my child to hold, to care for and protect, to teach and to please, to love forevermore. Burt, too, loves her infinitely and has from the time he held her, barely one week old, and walked her patiently back and forth for hours to stop her from crying as she grabbed on to his chest with her little fingers. She is fiercely his daughter too.

For better or for worse, she is of this generation. I wanted her to have my ideals, ethics, joys, and strengths, only what is good from me. This was always impossible and is one of life's cruelties for all mothers.

We are sitting around the pool, my husband and I, separated to let me enjoy the sun while he reads his newspapers in the shade. Out comes a pretty blonde girl, maybe a year younger than Rachel. She removes her wrap with great care and sits herself next to my husband, sharing his space. Is that what Rachel will become, seeking a man—doesn't matter who he is, doesn't matter where he is from, doesn't matter whom he belongs to? I hate this generation. I know the basic truths remain the same: Thou shalt not steal, thou shalt not commit adultery, thou shalt not covet thy neighbor's wife (or husband). I know this as a fact, no matter what society has come to with its movies and books and TV personalities and shows. I find flirting with strangers unacceptable, but then I am me, a person with principles and ethics and goals. In all the time Burt and I were seeing each other, five years to be exact, we respected each other without question. Our bodies were a temple given to us by God and our parents, not to be violated; that was obvious to both of us. My mother and I never spoke about such things; there was no time and certainly no occasion. Yet I knew this by instinct, and I hoped that this instinct would be passed to Rachel, by osmosis maybe, and by DNA.

I watch the girl's posturing, walking around, giving a furtive glance toward my husband to see if he is noticing her graceful figure, her pretty face. I hate this generation. Is there hope for my Rachel?

August 24

We drive around like there is no tomorrow to buy things Rachel "needs." We promised her a color TV, a carpet to replace the one we left behind, a lamp, some clothes and shoes, a hot plate, and a new Walkman to replace the one she got for her last birthday that no longer works. All the decisions we made last night go out the window. I wished to see a Japanese exhibit at the botanical gardens, Burt wanted to take a three-hour ride on the Mississippi, but here we are running from store to store. We can't seem to help ourselves. She has wound us around her little finger. We go for miles to accommodate our budget and her desires. We spend twice as much as what we planned, in three times the amount of time we had allotted. My head is spinning from all the driving around and all the purchases we have put on our credit cards. Burt is patient but has a pained expression on his face. We come back exhausted.

August 25

Today, all three of us do visit the botanical gardens where a Japanese festival is taking place. It is a feast for the eyes and ears—color, movement, and sound. We go to see old friends in the St. Louis Museum of Art: works by Monet, Braque, Picasso, a Van Gogh, some Klees and Mirós, a Jackson Pollock, a little gold sculpture by Degas, and the head of a muse by an American contemporary. We return by way of the stately mansions in the park, admiring the large boulevards flanked with lampposts that remind us so much of Paris. We see the famous Gateway Arch against a perfect blue sky, the baseball stadium downtown, and the unbelievable mosaics of the St. Louis Cathedral. We have had a good taste of the city and are ready to leave.

September 30, 1988

Dear Rachel,

I wish you a very happy birthday once more this year, because you have reached a landmark, which should not just be celebrated with a drink of good wine, but which should be reflected upon with all seriousness, as it is your gateway to freedom, your entrance into a myriad of possibilities, all of which I wish for you to be good, bright, and happy.

    I have accumulated a few articles* from different magazines to send to you because you told me at one point in our phone conversations that I never talked seriously to you about some subjects. I wish to amend this herewith, not to tell you what to do, but to let you have some facts. I can't say that I don't care what you do. I am never going to be able to say that, as I wish for your happiness and good health always. How you arrive at that goal is now forevermore in your hands. Let the past be in the past, except that you build on its mistakes and derive pleasure from what you did right. That's all anyone can do.

With much love and good wishes,
Your mother

*Enclosed please find one such article.

My Turn

A Letter from Mother to Daughter on Her Coming of Age

I am writing you this letter in the event that I have not expressed my feelings and thoughts to you clearly on a certain subject, due to difficulties with the language and sensitivity of the subject to both speaker and listener alike, and due to a reluctance on my part to divulge innermost secrets of the heart. The subject is men.

I will be frank and pragmatic; it is my woman-to-woman talk with you, as you are about to enter a new stage in your life, as you are about to become a woman, a creature mysterious and alluring to the opposite sex, the weaker partner perhaps, but the one in control of her destiny!

I hope you will take time out from your busy schedule to read this letter. I only wish to express my views clearly. There is no telling you what to do; the time for that has long since passed. I wish the best for you, but you make the choices. I know that you think that I am hopelessly old-fashioned, but after all, the proof is in the pudding: All my friends have been happily married for many years; all yours are still struggling to get there.

I start with a word of caution: A survey has been recently conducted and reported on in all the newspapers which claims, that young males will say anything for a little fun, while females are looking for sincerity and commitment in *every relationship*. Due to this basic truth, which, by the way, fits to any age, going to bed with someone for social reasons is a foolish thing to do for any young woman—it exposes her to heartache and pain and gives no reward. You take the risks, while he will have accomplished his goal. On the other hand, when a young man wishes to build a relationship, he will continue to seek you out even and especially if you refuse his advances. If he doesn't, you know for sure he was after some temporary fun and isn't worth the bother, an easy test you can apply again and again. So, if *you* make the rules, you can play the game *your* way.

To rephrase: Affairs end in broken hearts and worse, while friendships endure.

That brings me to the other matter I wish to discuss: how to choose a husband. Husbands are more precious than diamonds and the finest of gold, they are rare and unique and therefore to be selected most carefully. Remember the song "For Papa make him a scholar, for Mama make him as rich as a king, for me, why, I wouldn't holler, if he were handsome as anything…" But the most important thing in choosing a husband is that he be your friend. A friend is he who sees to your good all of the time, who doesn't play Russian roulette with your health. A friend is he who stands by you and loves you no matter what your shortcomings, a friend is he whom you love and stand by no matter what his faults. A friend is what you should seek before anything else; when you have a friend, everything else will fall into place.

I wish you such a friend with all my heart, and in the meantime, choose wisely whom you consort with, play the game well and be a real woman: Exciting, alluring, full of smartness and mystery!

We visited Rachel often as we had done throughout her college career, and we grew as fond of St. Louis as we had been of Boston and its environs.

In medical school, she became seriously interested in a young man in her class who was enrolled as a medical student. As he wasn't also pursuing a PhD, he would graduate several years before her, and that became a major problem. Under the guise of hating the person in whose lab she was assigned to work, she said she wanted to quit the

PhD program even though Burt counseled her to just apply for another sponsor more to her liking. Well, she insisted, and Burt appealed to the dean, who by chance was a colleague and respected friend. He counseled Burt to just give in and agree to her wishes. Nothing else would work! So she dropped out of the program and became a medical student only, whose parents now had to assume tuition. Poorer financially and rather upset from the arguing and the knowledge that she was making a mistake, we tried to put on a good face. We finally consoled ourselves with the fact that, after all, one can be a medical doctor and still do research.

She graduated in four years, and we were as proud as we could be. She was then accepted at Barnes-Jewish Hospital, St. Louis, as a resident, and that was the end of her relationship with the young man, who went on to a hospital in Boston. For him she had forfeited a prestigious PhD and some very substantial monies from our pocketbook.

She did well in her various rotations and decided to specialize in pediatrics. She spent a year in a Philadelphia children's hospital and then applied and obtained a fellowship at an institute in Memphis, St. Jude's Children Research Hospital. She had decided to go into the most difficult specialty of all, pediatric oncology and hematology. It did not take long before she finagled herself into a lab there, and she also began to do some clinical research. She had come full circle as far as her studies were concerned; she was a budding MD but also on her way to becoming a bona fide researcher. We eventually even had the joy of publishing a scientific paper authored by the three of us.

She lived in a cute little house and adopted a cute little dog from a shelter, which for her was a dream come true. She had wanted a dog for ages. We visited her in Memphis often, and the dog, named Panda because he was mostly white with some black patches, became part of the family.

BURT

I love my husband with all my heart and all my soul. We were now married for more than twenty-five years, and still, whenever I got home before him to prepare dinner, and he came through the door, my heart jumped for joy as I saw his face. Whenever the phone rang, and I heard his voice, happiness suffused me. Nothing has changed in those twenty-five years, only that I love him more deeply. When I walk down the street at his side, I am overcome with pride that he had chosen me. When we are in a crowd, I still seek him out with a glance again and again to rejoice in his presence. The fine lines of his face are chiseled like granite into my being. I love my husband more than my life.

We were married, two innocents, from worlds apart. His childhood had been toy trains and model airplanes, his youth consumed by school, baseball, collecting books to satisfy his insatiable curiosity, then work and building a career. My childhood and youth were lost in the sole purpose of surviving the Holocaust. My past was all pain. We met, and he introduced me to the joys of living. I see the sun rise, flowers grow; I see his world. He liked my rapt listening to his interminable talks, my fascination with every experience in his company. The years have flown by. I have had the joys and pain of raising a child, of earning a living, of learning and teaching, all with the happiness of him being beside me, giving me strength and support, and sharing my love despite some hurdles I put in his path. I love Burt more than my life. He has given me everything I treasure.

Occasionally, people ask me if I mind playing second fiddle to Burt in the scientific world as most think that it is all his ideas and his work that matter in the end. To them I say, "I have the best of all worlds. I am free to do what I want to do, I have a listening ear at my disposal at all times for my own brainstorms, I am privy to the best of conversations—and best of all, I don't have to write grants all by myself, a job that is thankless and daunting. So who cares what people think!"

TRAVEL ADVENTURES AND OTHER MATTERS

When Rachel was very young, we took her along to scientific meetings. Early on, the conferences important to us were held in Atlantic City. It was an easy drive from New York, and the lectures were convenient to go to. The hotels in which the meetings took place were all within walking distance of one another. When her father was scheduled to talk, I would take her into the meeting room, and Rachel would sit quietly, proudly watching her dad up on the podium. I also took her to social activities, like playing Ping-Pong, shuffleboard, and beach parties with other children of the group. Later when she got older, I stayed at home while Burt traveled, staying away just long enough to learn the latest scientific progress and to deliver his talks. As Rachel progressed to college and medical school and beyond, we again traveled together and kept in touch with her regularly on the telephone and by writing long letters.

When Burt and I traveled, I would take along two notebooks: one to take notes of the science and another, using it as a diary to record our travel adventures so I would not forget any of the details of the sightseeing or anything of importance and worth remembering, separate from the science. I was fascinated with everything. Being able to travel freely was so special to me, no matter how tired and harried I sometimes got. I always rejoiced in the freedom accorded to me by my precious blue passport, which I took great pride in. At such times, I could not forget how difficult it all used to be for my parents and me, no matter how hard I tried to push it into the background.

So I have copied some of the trips Burt and I took from the diary, word for word, proof of the privilege of being an American citizen and what wondrous adventures this brought about, and always with the unique ability of coming back home. I have done this despite my worries that I might bore the reader, who I hope will forgive the indulgence.

October 2, 1988

Burt is invited by the Chinese government via Dr. Huang, one of my favorite colleagues who spent more than a year in our lab, to come and give some lectures in several medical schools, and I am invited too. I am more reluctant than usual to come along. I know their financial situation relative to their population is not the greatest, and for China to spend so much money on me I find uncomfortable. But Burt is somewhat apprehensive to go it alone—too many miles to cover, too much jet lag to overcome. I am also worried about Rachel—she has her first midterm exams in medical school this coming week, and we are adding to her anxiety by flying off to China. She claims it is unfair of us and that we could have gone a week later. I am filled with remorse.

We arrive in Los Angeles and are greeted by a balmy atmosphere. I am not soothed. LA is an old friend, no need to explore it. We rest near the airport in preparation for the next flight to Honolulu. I scan in my mind a picture I have on a wall in my office, a painting called *Misty Rain*. I dwell on the gentle curves, the calming dark green, gray, and black, the quiet beauty of form and the emotion it brings forth. My mind's eye proceeds to the bold Chinese writing I have hung up next to the picture. The large black lettering is as mysterious as the country I am about to visit. My Chinese friends all have wonderful faces molded by superior, unassuming intelligence. I love all things Chinese: the delicate designs, the blue and white colors, the mysterious intricate writing, the gentle quiet scrolls, the long wonderful history of knowledge, science, mathematics. But visiting China had never been in my travel plans.

When I ask Burt what he thinks about China, he responds: "Flowing rivers, magic mountains, forbidden cities, mysterious people." He has wished to see China for a long, long time. He can hardly contain his excitement.

We will be staying in Honolulu for one day and night. Am I going to dismiss Oahu and its sister islands as I did LA? We have taken many happy trips to Hawaii—four meetings, and one combined with a real vacation. The glorious weather has never let us down: constant sunshine, interrupted occasionally by a momentary sprinkling of rain. From the air, the islands appear like granite carvings in the blue ocean, and Burt remarks for the fifth time what a wonder it is that the pilot finds the small dots in all this vastness of water. I recognize Pearl Harbor then see Waikiki Beach and Diamond Head.

As we deplane, my senses are overwhelmed—the sweet smell of flowers, a pure blue sky, warm balmy air, hills stretched out in the background like lace against the sky, and green vegetation. Palm trees with their slim tall trunks slightly curving, people in colorful Hawaiian shirts—I can't resist the place. Slowly but surely, happiness fills me again, and I leave my worries behind.

The desk clerk at the hotel gives us a seaside room on the thirty-sixth floor. We are greeted with a fragrant bouquet of flowers and a bottle of champagne. The view is breathtaking: the green-blue ocean with rippling white foam near the shore, Waikiki Beach with its majestic hotels stretched out for miles, a few boats, a catamaran, a blue sky with a few flighty clouds hanging on the hills. We have just one day in this paradise; tomorrow it's onward.

We have lunch before a waterfall in the hotel lobby. I sip a smoothie, the taste of pure nectar; some Hawaiian boys play the guitar. I walk down the street—a myriad of shops, a woman's paradise: everywhere are black and pink coral, glistening opals, dark-blue lapis lazuli stones and green jades; colorful clothes with the imprints of hibiscus and orchids. I send Rachel some chocolate-covered macadamia nuts and select a few postcards. I try to take it all in, wade in the ocean, and fight the jet lag with a cup of Kona coffee and half of a papaya, food that affects me like incense.

We call the mainland and talk to Rachel; she is excited having established Bitnet communication with her beloved former college lab colleagues. She adds that school is the best, her teachers are super; they can't do enough for the students. She then can't help but mention once again that she is overcome by the enormous amount of material she needs to learn. We sympathize and tell her for the twentieth time she does not need to know it all, just enough to pass her tests this first term. We promise to call again the same time next day and sign off as friends.

October 4

We arrive at the airport, and Burt realizes that we will be in midair at the time we promised to call Rachel. It is one day before her first exam, and we can't reach her. I get upset, and Burt produces the telephone number of the residence hall she lives in. I tell the woman who answers of our predicament, and she promises to place a note in Rachel's mailbox. I wonder if Rachel will receive the message in time, but I am reassured, having met the lady. I remember her beautiful brown skin, high cheekbones, smiling face, and friendly demeanor. To explain my reasoning: a fellow I watched on TV once (on a rare instant I turned on the idiot box) said that all whites are prejudiced against blacks. I got up indignantly that day and cursed the fellow out—was I not white? How could he say such a thing? I judge people by the way they treat me, and I have had nothing but good from the African-American people around me. First there was that secretary who suggested to Burt that he take me out for a date; with that she gave me all that is best in my life. Then, as we work in a predominantly black neighborhood, I have had plenty of chances for interaction. There is the dean of medical students, a kindly man whom Burt likes to talk with. I see him often in the halls, conversing easily with the students, putting them at ease, calming worried minds. Then there is the library, with maybe two or three whites on the staff; the rest are black, and I love them all. The library is an essential part of my existence, and there is nothing this staff would not do for me to help me out. They bend the rules a little, letting me borrow a book longer than is normally allowed; when I can't find some material myself, they search tirelessly for me to a point beyond the call of duty, and sometimes they make kindly conversation with me when I appear harried and distressed. Then there is one of our research assistants, a man from Ethiopia, who has been with us for almost twenty years. He is the nearest thing to a brother I have. We treat each other like family, he and I. He can do anything required of him and do it well, so he is our right hand, indispensable to our research. I ask his advice on family matters, too, because he has a kind, gentle, optimistic attitude that serves me well. In return, I occasionally have to push him to assert himself in financial dealings, when his timidity gets in the way. We trust each other and care for each other. Then there is the cleaning man from whom I get a cheerful "Hi, Doc" each morning, along with extra paper towels, a clean room, and whatever is needed to discard chemicals, broken glass, and other objects. He takes it all off my hands with a friendly smile.

In contrast to this milieu, we live in a white neighborhood. I have not one good word to say about that other than the views from our apartment are great since we face a river and bridge, and Rachel's schools were good. The people I have come to dislike. We were subject to twenty-one years of unkindness—no hellos, no holding doors, and worst of all, no one to play with Rachel when she was small. She was never invited to anyone's home. It seemed that Rachel just was not good enough to play with those other kids. My pure white liberal lady neighbors were not my sisters.

Getting back to our trip, I keep my fingers crossed, pretty sure Rachel will get our message, and board United. The stewardesses are really friendly, as the commercial says, and I snuggle into my extra-wide seat bound for Hong Kong.

October 6

It is evening, and the airplane passes a row of what look like golden toy skyscrapers, neatly placed one next to another from the edge of a harbor up to the foot of gently undulating hills. We arrive in Hong Kong. The airport is unbelievably crowded. It seems impossible to find an exit, let alone a taxi. I cling to Burt for dear life. We push our way through the crowd and make it to an exit. The street is crowded too. We find a long line of people who seem to be waiting for transportation, so we join them and wait. At long last we make it into a taxi, which brings us to the best hotel on the island.

We wait to check in as the lobby is just as crowded as the street. I stand against a marble pole, lost in the crowd, while Burt makes his way slowly toward the desk. Finally, he checks in, and we are shown to an absolutely gorgeous room. I can't believe my eyes: all this sumptuous environment after the humdrum arrival and the long wait in the crowd. We wash up and go to the dining room, which has the grandest view ever. It is wall-to-wall window, from ceiling to floor. A panorama of modern skyscrapers spreads before us, tall and right up to the edge of the water with slim spaces in between. Each building has a different architecture. The water in front of them is teeming with the movement of boats, ferries, tankers, cargo ships, Chinese junks. On the other side of the water are skyscrapers again, starting at the shore and reaching toward the hills. It seems the very best architects have been at work here. Multifaceted, glittering towers seemingly completely made of glass give way to silvery metal buildings, on which the sun reflects the neighboring towers. Others have sharply angled walls of concrete with odd-shaped windows and odd-shaped tops. It is a feast to behold.

View from the dining room in the hotel in Hong Kong

Building in Hong Kong

Building in Hong Kong

Hong Kong is made up of several islands, and in the morning, we tour two islands by bus. The bus goes through streets with large, colorful advertising signs bearing the beautiful characters of Chinese writing in red and blue and white and gold and black. We pass through a tunnel from Kowloon to Hong Kong. The architecture of the commercial buildings is all breathtaking.

Soon we see the other side of this fairyland: the bus passes large apartment dwellings built of water-damaged brick that look ready to crumble, gray and morbid, every window crowded with laundry stretched over sticks to dry in the sun. Our guide explains that these low-cost government-built houses contain an average of four families per apartment: Hong Kong is the most crowded spot on earth. I am shocked by the poverty I see. The bus heads toward the water, and we take a ride in a "sand huck" (water taxi) among the boat people. These families live all their lives on the water, some in houseboats and others on fishing vessels. Most boats are steered by old women squatting on bent legs.

I am shaken, contrasting this poverty with the beauty we just left. These people live out their lives with no creature comfort whatsoever. The women crouch, fixing fish to be hung up to dry in the sun, their weather-beaten faces unsmiling as they do their incessant work.

For the crowded masses the government is constructing forty- to fifty-story buildings to be divided into tiny apartments. This should be an improvement over the constant fighting that goes on in the multi-family compounds, our guide says.

They work hard and long, these people, while I luxuriate in space and beauty, with good clean food and drink, freedom to move about, and time to waste. The bus tour has saddened me. I give a big tip to the guide, as if it could trickle down to a poverty-stricken boat dweller.

Water taxi in Hong Kong

Boat people from Hong Kong

Chinese junks in Hong Kong

October 7

We take a boat ride in the harbor and see more boat people at the foot of some of the new apartment buildings being constructed. We see enormous hotels and downtown Hong Kong. Getting off the boat, I cannot shake off the discomfort and hurt at the thought of the poverty of the people, and my usual enthusiasm for shopping has disappeared. As we walk along the streets and see all the jade and carved ivory, Chinese fans and artwork displayed in the shopping arcades, I cannot buy a single item. Rachel can do without.

The hotel cannot accommodate us for our last night in Hong Kong despite our reservation, so they help us move to another brand-new hotel, complete with a heated rooftop pool.

October 8

The next morning, I enjoy sunshine, soft breezes, and a long swim in the pool to soothe my soul while Burt looks over his lecture material: his slides and little slips of paper with key phrases. We depart for Beijing late in the evening via China Air. We stand in line to check in our luggage and have our passports and visas checked. Everything goes smoothly, except the buttons on my jacket set off the security alarm. I am mortified and have to be hand-scanned by a young attendant with a special device. The moment passes, and we enter a 747 that is filled to the last seat. October is one of the busiest times for this lap of our journey. After three hours of smooth flight and a meal consisting of rice, duck, and a piece of cake, we arrive. Dr. Huang is there to greet us with one of his assistants. They grab our luggage and whisk us off in a private car to what looks like a rather shabby hotel. (The lady who made the reservations had never done this before, and Dr. H is embarrassed, but we reassure him that it is okay.) We are to be ready at 5:30 the next morning for our flight to Nanchang.

Strange figures walk about in the hallway in the dark, staring at us. Inside, the room has three narrow cots, a Thermos filled with hot water, and two cups covered with lids. There is a sink whose water pipes leak in three places. Burt refuses to get undressed or even undo his belt. He is dismayed but falls asleep immediately due to the lateness of the hour and emotional exhaustion. I keep my clothes on too, listen to the gnawing noises of some animal in one corner of the room, but fall asleep.

October 9

At 5:00 a.m., there is a knock on the door. We waken and brush our teeth with Coca-Cola we had left over from the trip. We head back to the airport in the dark with a shriveled ego. We miss our creature comforts, a clean environment, and fresh air that have become essential to us. I remember Hong Kong and sit quietly in the airplane seat reproaching myself. We are on our way to southern China in a full plane. Burt sheepishly tells me China will be a lesson in humility. We take to the air, shaken and unsure of ourselves and longing for home. My window seat allows me to see an amazing display: winding rivers that shimmer in the sun, rippled hills and mountains with shapes I have never seen before. There is a magical quality to them. Small and large water bodies that reflect the sun like mirrors. More gracefully curved winding rivers, many of them narrow but one majestically wide, the famous Yangtze River, which I learned about in high school years ago. I am consoled by the sights below me and a presweetened cup of black coffee.

Mountains in China

We arrive in Nanchang. A friend of Dr. H's meets us, and we enter a taxi. What I see on the road does little to inspire me with confidence in what lies ahead. The road is dusty and crowded with bicycles on either side. We ride in a two-way lane, trucks and buses intermingled with no apparent speed limit. Our driver races to overcome whatever vehicle is ahead of him, barely making it back to his side of the road to avoid oncoming traffic. He is ruthless to bicycles and cars alike and uses his horn incessantly. Alongside the road are hovels that serve as habitation. People sit on the bare sidewalk displaying wares for sale. Women are pulling heavy loads of wood and bricks on carts; on their shoulders, some are balancing two pails hanging on either side of a bamboo stick. The poverty I see is appalling. I was not prepared for this. Nanchang is crowded with poor people. The city streets abound with vendors. Some have little pushcarts on which they cook meals, served on plates that have not been washed, and drinks are poured in glasses that have not been rinsed from one use to the next. I have heard that hepatitis is endemic in this region.

The hotel we are assigned to is old, but we have been given a suite of two well-furnished rooms and a bathroom. The plumbing is leaking and the tub is rusty, but the rooms are quite stately. The food we are treated to is tasty and plentiful. There are many dishes in succession, and the soup is served last. We repeatedly, but surreptitiously, wipe our plates with napkins because it seems the dishes are not washed with soap. In fact, soap is a rare commodity here; the floors are swept with sawdust by long, whisk-like brooms made of straw. Imagine no Joy or Ivory or any of the many soapy liquids, scented or unscented, we take for granted. I vow to send a bottle of dishwashing liquid to each of my new lady friends. We brush our teeth with mineral water. Burt is dying for a shower, but I forbid him to go near the tub.

We meet the people at the medical college. They are gentle people, immediately warm as they receive us with unquestioning kindness. The classrooms are ancient, no fresh paint on the walls, metal benches and tabletops that lift up. The hallways are dark, the labs small and cluttered, the floors unwashed. But I love the people. The students look at us with admiration and smile, greeting us with cheerful hellos.

Burt lectures admirably. After each sentence, he pauses for the translator, who bows slightly to signal the end of each translation. Burt never loses his thread despite having no written text. I am proud of his ability and of the nice way he ends his talk by acknowledging our hosts, the translator, and the young man showing Burt's slides.

We are invited to a luncheon party near a beautiful, large lake, the pride of Nanshang, with the faculty and students. It is a banquet unlike any I have ever experienced. A procession of dishes, fifteen if I've counted correctly, adorn a large lazy Susan in the middle of the table. We all help ourselves with chopsticks and porcelain spoons. There are delicacies of fish, squid, pork, duck, frogs' legs, deep-fried shrimp, crayfish, noodles and rice, two kinds of vegetables, pineapple, and, finally, soup. The sumptuous meal and the beauty of the place are somewhat incongruous with what we've seen of the city. But I am happy for the people in the school, who work long and hard hours with scarce materials and little help, but still accomplish a lot.

We next visit another treasure of the city, "The Eight Mountain People's" home. It is a series of old wooden houses with much artwork on display, scrolls of delicate paintings and scriptures, nestled among restful gardens. The place has many visitors, mostly young schoolchildren cavorting about. Some bid us hello and run off with laughter. It is a pavilion of ancient times, a remembrance of a people who are now extinct.

October 10

We return to Beijing. The way to the city from the airport is lined on both sides with beautiful weeping willow trees. The traffic is thick again, with bicycles on both sides of the road. Some streets are wider and actually have bicycle lanes. There is smog in the air, but the climate is mild. There are modern apartment houses, many with balconies. This time, we are assigned a suite with a bathroom in a nice hotel. The water keeps running here too, but only in the bathtub. The hotel is located in an area full of construction of new high-rise buildings.

We are off to see the Forbidden City: courtyard upon courtyard, building upon building—golden ceilings, multicolored walls, nine thousand rooms in all, a vast expanse of similar colors and similar shapes. Droves of people visit this city. We see thrones and intricate furnishings, carvings and lanterns, screens and mirrors, silk-covered beds, dragons carved in stone, the symbol of the emperor on the floor. Two large carved Chinese lions guard the gates of the buildings: a male with one paw on a ball, a female with a cub. The film *The Last Emperor* does not quite capture the expanse of the Imperial Palace. We climb a hill and can see the whole of the Forbidden City and the whole of Beijing.

Burt is invited to give a lecture at Beijing University. We are graciously received and then invited by the host to a lunch party. We go to a restaurant in a fine Beijing shopping street lined with antique shops. The restaurant owner, who claims to be a descendant of Confucius, serves us a banquet of pigeon eggs, meats, chicken, duck, shrimp and fish, vegetables and rice, sweet-and-sour soup, and fruit. We have our own room decorated with colorful lanterns, and I am struggling with chopsticks to decrease the amount of food I eat. We say farewell and many thanks and are off to the Summer Palace.

Green and blue and gold and orange cloisonné decorates pavilions on hills, in gardens on a wide beautiful lake; seventeen boats lined up to form a bridge lead there, some are dragon-shaped with yellow roofs. It is the dowager empress's favorite place. I concur with her taste.

The Summer Palace in Beijing

People in Beijing seem much better off than those in the south. The buildings are modern and well kept. Yet on the streets, many bicycles are loaded down with goods, and the buses are crowded to capacity, standing room only, with some holding on to the handles of the doors, riding on outside steps. Long lines of people wait at each bus stop, and the people work long hours; we see them in the middle of the night working at construction sites and paving streets.

Burt gives a lecture in the school of our host, Dr. Huang, who has taken us around every step of the way. He has made sure that the lecture hall is packed. The students are eager to talk with me. Smiling and friendly, they ask good-natured questions. They look young and vulnerable, bright and eager. No makeup, no frilly hairdos, plain-clothed and clean-scrubbed. They seem so well-adjusted and sure of themselves despite their halting English, ready to laugh at my feeble pleasantries. They are in another world, another era, unspoiled by too-easy living and too many possessions. Respectful and friendly, they are people after my own heart.

The Lion guarding the Palace in the Forbidden City in Beijing

The Lion in front of the Palace in the Forbidden City, Beijing

A Palace in the Forbidden City

October 11

We visit a brand-new research institute headed by a bright, elderly lady. She shows us each department. We meet and talk to scientists who tell us briefly of their latest endeavors. I am impressed by the modern approach to traditional medicine. Burt is impressed by the equipment. There is talk of genetics and immunology, cardiovascular and nervous diseases, Chinese herbs and their active ingredients, which are now being eagerly sought in Japan and the US. The scientists look hardworking, serious, and poor. "I fear for China"—this phrase, which I heard long ago, keeps echoing in my mind. They treat us so royally. I feel pained and wish to withdraw, take myself home, not to disturb their eager striving, since I am not in a position to help their needs.

October 14

Burt gives another lecture, and we are invited to a luncheon by the head of the school. We find ourselves in a noisy establishment—the guests next to us keep toasting each other with glasses filled with what must be pretty strong wine. The host is somewhat embarrassed due to the noise, but I enjoy the spontaneous, uninhibited fun. We wade through another banquet of fish, fowl, meat, and vegetables, rice and soup, cookies and steamed balls of bread. My digestive system is about to rebel, and I beg off an evening tour of the city to rest and be restored.

Life in the hotel is a hustle and bustle of tours coming from other parts of China, Europe and the US. I hear German, French, Swedish, Polish and English.

October 15

Burt is off to see the Great Wall of China and a Ming Dynasty tomb. I ask to be excused. As eager as I am to sightsee, I cannot have another luncheon party and then be ready for a meal our dear host has been promising to treat us to in his home. It is a big honor to be invited there, and I wish to be rested and be able to enjoy the many delicacies he has been describing to us, which will be cooked by his wife, who is a scientist too and spent several months in our lab. Our host's wife is a fragile and beautiful lady who looks like a Chinese porcelain figurine. So I have only a light breakfast of coffee and toast (the only Western food the hotel provides), take a walk to a nearby shop and purchase a few trinkets made in cloisonné style in the colors of the Summer Palace, to bring to Rachel and some friends. Then I go back to sit in the lobby to lazily watch the comings and goings and sip a cup of great-tasting coffee. I take another walk and end up in the most famous hotel in Beijing, a huge construction of glass and metal. The tourists here are mostly Germans and Americans. The enormous lobby is decorated to promote the Oktoberfest, a German celebration. There is appropriate "oompah" music, and droves of overdressed patrons pass to and fro. I reflect on the fact that I could not possibly come to this country to sightsee in this fashion, although it is surely good for the economy. Then I go back and get ready for the dinner party.

The Great Wall of China

Burt and I walk up six flights of stairs. The halls are dark, the walls in need of a coat of paint. We enter and see three sparsely furnished rooms full of smiling faces, the grown daughter of our host and hostess, her husband and some post-doctoral fellows, all eager to please. We are given the seats of honor and are formally greeted. Then our hostess starts bringing dishes from the kitchen, one at a time, lovingly prepared and very delicious. The hostess does not have a minute to talk, but she smiles at us and keeps bringing more tasty food. She manages to place many different delicacies on an average-size coffee table, and there is still room for our little serving plates and glasses filled with some ambrosia available only in China. We have a pleasant conversation. A translating graduate student helps those who are not fluent in English.

After the lengthy meal, we are presented with gifts: a beautiful amber necklace for me, an exquisite tie tack for Burt. I have been successfully fighting off their desire to buy us presents during our sightseeing, other than some postcards, apples, and persimmons. We are embarrassed but have to accept this last token of their solicitous kindness. We leave to return to the hotel, thanking everyone for their flawless hospitality.

October 17

Dear Rachel,

The last day of our trip has been most grueling. In the morning, Daddy gave another lecture and then there was a luncheon party prepared by the graduate students, followed by an open seminar in which the students could ask questions. There were about ten students for each of us, each one eager to learn how to get a job in the US. They were all so sweet, innocent, and eager, it was hard to tell them the blunt facts—like you have to pass exams, or there is no space in our laboratory at the moment.

At 3:00 p.m., we were rushed off in a car to see the main square in Beijing. We got back to our hotel at 4:15, and Daddy said he wanted desperately to lie down and rest. No sooner did he take off his shirt than there was a knock on the door. It turned out that the lady who had made the hotel reservation for us (the same one as when we'd arrived) told them we needed the room until the seventeenth, which is correct day-wise but not night-wise. So here we were, dead tired, and we had to pack all our things—a considerable feat, what with the clothes, five hundred slides, innumerable scientific papers, breakable Chinese presents. Daddy became his stubborn self and announced that he would not go to the university president's dinner party, scheduled for 6:00 p.m., until we had another room. Meanwhile, two graduate students who had accompanied us on this outing and the manager of the hotel argued loudly in the hallway in front of our room the whole time we were packing, forty-five minutes in all. I was in acute agony knowing that the dinner party was a must and that punctuality was also a must. The hotel manager told us to check our bags in the check room and wait in the lobby.

I managed to convince Daddy with threats of killing myself to go to the dinner party, room or not. At about 5:30, we were told that there would be a room for us at 7:00 p.m. Daddy conceded to go to the dinner party, and so we went, not having changed our clothes from the morning, not even having washed our hands. We arrived at the banquet a few minutes late. We were from then until the end of the evening treated like official representatives of the US, seated on each side of the president of the university with three high officials of the Health Department on Daddy's other side, our professor host and his graduate student to do the translations on my other side. Sentence by sentence, the president slowly spoke then his words were translated into English. Then Daddy spoke a sentence, and it was translated into Chinese while the rest of us sat in complete silence. It was totally formal. Every once in a while, the president made a toast and we all got up, touched glasses, and sipped some wine. In the meanwhile, a large lazy Susan in the middle of the table was loaded with dishes and spun around. The president took some food every so often from the dish with his chopsticks and placed it on Daddy's plate and my plate, and we dutifully ate—cold meats, cold chicken, and pickled cucumbers to start; a hot dish of meat, fish, spicy rice, and Chinese cabbage with mushrooms. Then came Peking duck, which is to be eaten as follows: You take a pancake with your fingers off a plate, place on it a green vegetable dipped in a brown sauce, then take two pieces of duck and roll the pancake. You then eat this with your fingers. It is quite delicious if you happen to be hungry. Then we ate soup and finally a piece of watermelon. I was stuffed to the gills to say the least. We subsequently got up for a final toast, which had to be bottoms up, and a formal presentation of a plaque and two exquisite Chinese vases. Then we started to the door and exchanged formal farewells. Daddy acted throughout the dinner like an accomplished diplomat. He chose just the right words, said just the right pleasantries, quoted from history and geography, and was altogether charming. You would have been proud of him.

We proceeded out and found that our driver had not returned from another job, so we were driven in the president's car, while he and his companions waited to go home, another embarrassing moment. In the hotel, it being now quite late, we got our luggage out of storage and went to our new room while our professor host and the graduate student sat down to say their formal farewells. While they were talking, Daddy pointed to a large cockroach that was taking a leisurely walk near his head on the wall. Professor H. was unperturbed and continued, laboriously recounting all our virtues and abilities, and how we came to China, and how we should have stayed much longer, and how we would proceed together in friendship and conquer new frontiers in science. He then brought forth thirty-six pictures he had taken of us and a load of new presents. I was about to dissolve of embarrassment and fatigue when the telephone rang announcing a visitor, a lady who fervently wanted to come to our lab but was not in the good graces of our host. She was in the lobby to make her farewells. She came up to our room, stayed for a little while, presented us with some gifts, and left without being able to talk about what she had come for.

At long last, we bid our gracious host and student good-bye and tried to go to bed. As we opened our bags, Daddy discovered another huge cockroach, and another and another. He started to scream at me, as to be expected, and I saw no way out other than to complain to the management—the roaches were all over, and they were enormous. We went to the housekeeper but could not make ourselves understood. We then went to the front desk and the attendant too did not understand our words but was willing to come up and see the problem. We showed him and he said okay, we should wait, he would send the housekeeper with some medicine. We sat for a while, our flesh crawling, and then could not take it anymore, so we proceeded down to see the manager about another room. The manager asked us politely to kindly spell the words *insect*, *bug*, and *cockroach* for him in case the problem came up again and then to wait in his office, the hotel being pretty full.

After some time and a lot of telephone calls on his part, he told us he had found a small room for us. Daddy insisted on inspecting it first, so we went up and to my utter dismay saw a fine room with another two giant cockroaches. Daddy tried to start up again, but I put my foot down and told him since there were only two instead of a whole army, we should take the room as I was way past exhaustion. We moved our luggage, left all the lights on, and crawled into bed without opening our bags, without even so much as brushing our teeth. I slept for a while, then woke and felt utterly miserable. I looked around, killed one roach in the bathroom, and lay awake thinking I would surely not make it home again, having no energy left. I finally fell asleep once more.

Now here I am in this beautiful silvery bird, a United plane, homeward bound, to my beloved country. See you soon. Love, The Wanderers

We had been the first lab group to have scientists come from China to our university system to work in the US. In all, four senior scientists came from one famous university in Beijing, stayed for several years with us, and returned to their school. One postdoc came to work with us too and stayed in the US. After our extensive trip to China and their so very gracious hosting, the higher-ups of the Chinese university decided to collaborate with our school and have Burt be the liaison in an extended exchange program of scientists and postdocs, and in addition, to send over different herbs they had studied and found to be effective against certain diseases. Our university would be engaged in analyzing the herbs to find the active ingredients responsible for their beneficial effects. We were honored and excited about the plan, but when it came time for the elite of the Beijing University to visit our school, the president of our university refused to greet them or even see them. He sent an underling to say that we were not going to be in a position to accommodate them or work with them. We were dumbfounded. Since Burt never was part of the "inner circle," we never found out the reason for this outcome. We were very embarrassed and "lost face," but even worse, our university lost a great financial boon, since the collaboration was all going to be paid for by China.

Sometime later, the monies and studies went to two well-known pharmaceutical firms and the National Institutes of Health.

Dr. H, who was the mover and shaker of the plan, remained friends with us, and the young man who had remained in the US for the sole purpose of helping implement the arrangement stayed in our lab for several more years.

GOING ON VACATION
AFTER WRITING A GRANT

Two months after the in-many-ways exhilarating but exhausting China trip and weeks of hard work, we decided to take a real vacation with Rachel. On December 17, 1988, Rachel's first break from medical school will begin, and Burt has decided to use all the free tickets and free rooms we have coming to us through the frequent-flyer system and the Marriott Stays program to go to California to places we have not been to before.

Burt has been writing a proposal for a much-needed grant since we are running out of funds to do research with, and it is almost zero hour. Everything is coming to an end, all our research; not a penny for my salary or that of our two postdocs will be left. To me, it is a catastrophe; but to Burt, it is simply one more challenge to overcome. Writing a grant is a rather unpleasant task and tends to be left, at least by us, to the very last minute. It entails much brainwork, much repetition to show that you know what you are talking about, and precision of facts down to the last word.

Writing a grant has to show that (1) the work you intend to do is a logical outgrowth of some experiments done before, (2) you have generated some preliminary data proving the soundness of the concepts you propose to investigate, (3) the work is novel, (4) there exists literature in peer-reviewed journals pointing to the need to do the experiments proposed, and (5) you have familiarity with the advanced technology to be used. You also must (6) mention the personnel that will carry it out, (7) indicate the money needed for equipment and salaries down to the last dollar and (8) prove you have the lab space required to do the work.

Burt has been writing fast and furious, but there is no end in sight. The t's have to be crossed and the i's dotted, and everything has to be rehashed what seems like one hundred times. The repetitiousness irks me as I reread for the tenth time what he has given me to correct and shorten. It seems impossible to meet the deadline as there are two days to go and ten sections to finish. I am upset as Burt is writing away, and the secretaries give us big eyes of distrust, wondering how long this work is going to be this time as they have seen this "condition red" many times before. I am losing all my patience with Burt. How can he still be writing steadfastly? Who is going to be able to go over this monstrous tome, and who is going to be able to type it? A friend and colleague, who is coprincipal investigator, comes to my aid and tries to keep the peace between Burt and me. He is actually an amazing force. He is able to shorten what Burt would not allow me to touch and calm us down individually. Still, it is a touch-and-go situation.

The day before the deadline, we rent a room in the city to continue to work to all hours and be able to get to work early. The night before we are to leave for California, we realize the trip has to be postponed by at least one day. The grant proposal is still not finished, let alone edited, typed, and xeroxed fifteen times. I have had no lunch or dinner. The next day, the three of us, and one saintly secretary who has agreed to stay, work at an even pace until 3:15 in the morning. I am totally and utterly exhausted. Burt and Dr. B are even able to crack a joke or two while they place the required copies of the finished grant in the mailbox at the main post office and we get home at 4:15 a.m. I fall into bed.

The next day, after four loads of laundry and half an hour to pack later, we get to the airport with three minutes to spare. I am overwrought. Burt has lost his cool too; though we changed our reservations, we still have our old tickets with yesterday's departure on them, and the man at the ticket desk claims the plane has been closed. Still, he takes our bags, and we literally run to the gate, arriving as the last few people are leisurely boarding. Burt's face relaxes, and I sheepishly take my seat near the window, fasten my seat belt, and we are on our way. My nerves are raw as if stretched by a violin tuner. It is good we have five hours to perhaps relax before we meet Rachel at LAX. Will I be able to gather my brain cells together to weather whatever storm she might bring about? She just finished some final exams and is probably ready for a good drag-out fight with us. I am definitely not up to that. Burt is buried in one of the umpteen newspapers he has brought on board. I settle in with the Sunday *Times* crossword puzzle and pray for strength.

The plane ride on Pan Am is soothing and trouble-free. The food is good, the movie stupidly relaxing, and I am somewhat restored as we meet Rachel, who is looking totally green around the gills having had little sleep and little food for the past several days. I brace myself, and we proceed to Newport Beach and our first stop in a Marriott hotel. Our suite will give us just the right distance to avoid quarrels over TV-watching, light shining in one's eyes, and living and breathing space. It is a genius arrangement, and we all settle into a routine of lots of sleep, lots of food, and very serious shopping for new clothing for Rachel. Contentment settles in before we go sightseeing.

We wander around in the castle of San Simeon, and in the quaint town of San Luis Obispo, we see sea lions sunning themselves on rocks jutting out in the ocean. We visit the famous aquarium in San Diego. It is a delightful few days of togetherness.

A TRIP TO JAPAN: A TRIP LIKE NO OTHER

Or How Not to Go to Japan

As mentioned before, we had several senior scientists and some just starting out from various regions of Japan working in our lab to learn techniques and/or fulfill requirements for advancement in their careers. As usual, we became good friends, invited them into our home for parties, and stayed in touch with them. When back at home, several of the senior scientists invited both of us to come to their country to give some talks at their universities, and the younger ones invited us to visit their cities or homes so we could enjoy and get to know their country, to show us how grateful they were for our befriending them in the United States. In general, it is my opinion that the Japanese people tend to stay aloof and formal with strangers, so they must have been particularly impressed with our simple friendliness. In addition, there were some senior scientists who got to know Burt from various meetings, and they too invited us to present our work in detail. So we had invitations from several places, and Burt managed to combine a trip to Japan that would take us all over, but he did not tell me exactly what this would entail so as not to scare me off from the frantic schedule he had prepared. His method was to tell me as little as possible to get me to come along.

July 14, 1993

We have put in a full day's work instead of leaving early, and we have not packed a stitch or gotten ourselves together in any way. Even the presents I so hastily shopped for last weekend are not assembled or wrapped. It is a grave disaster as we enter our apartment at 7:30 p.m., hungry and tired and with all that work ahead of us. We gulp down some sandwiches and set to the task with me complaining the entire evening that I cannot possibly get this done. I throw all my favorite clothes into a valise and soon see that the bag cannot possibly accommodate them. I leave the unruly mess and turn to wrapping the gifts, one by one, till a giant bag is filled to capacity. It is 1:30 a.m. by the time I turn back to my clothes and grudgingly return many back to the closet. I settle for the bare minimum, all the while complaining. It is too late to choose jewelry and makeup, so I take it all and throw it into my tote, stuff some beach shoes and a pair of dress shoes into the valise, and try to force the bag closed. When I turn to look at Burt, he is struggling to close a bag that must weigh a ton. Besides that, he has one full tote bag with about five hundred slides, a briefcase filled to capacity, and newspapers and other reading material in an oversize shopping bag. It is 2:30 a.m., and no time to argue, since we have to get up at 5:00 if we hope to make the plane on time with our caravan of bags.

Two hours later, I have to shake Burt to get him awake. We have a quick breakfast and are still trying to force the bags closed, half-dressed, when the taxi driver rings our intercom. We beg for ten more minutes and manage to settle into the cab fifteen minutes later, huffing and puffing and red in the face, as the cab driver explains that he will have to charge us for the extra time and the many bags. It is not a good omen, but the ride to the airport is uneventful, and once we get rid of our two large suitcases, we somehow manage to stash the four giant tote bags onto a luggage carrier and are each left with one shopping bag to carry. Burt, his usual self, wants to make a last-minute change with the tickets so we can visit Rachel on our way back to New York, but after some lengthy negotiations and my increasing unease as to the time wasted, he decides to give it up because the expense is exorbitant. I heave a sigh of relief, and off we go to board the plane. After an inhuman struggle to squeeze our various totes and jackets and carry bags into a space, we settle into an oversize first-class seat complete with footrest, pillow, blanket, television, and musical program. For the first time in weeks of anticipation, I relax as the stewardess presses a glass of juice into my hand.

July 15

We arrive in Los Angeles and spend some time shopping for more presents for all our friends in Japan.

July 16

We arrive in Honolulu.

July 17

Dear Rachel,

Hawaii is as beautiful as ever. I could stay here for a month breathing this wonderful air and feeling the soft warmth of the climate, like no other. But we are leaving for Guam tomorrow. It was fun talking to you this morning. I went swimming at 6:30 a.m. The hotel is great and all the outdoor stands are still here, but no shopping for us today. It is more fun to just sit in the sun. Love, The Travelers

July 18+1

Dear Rachel,

We had a seven-and-a-half-hour flight to get to Guam, but arrived three hours later the next day. Don't ask me to explain this. Daddy made a giant-size scene when we got to the airport to leave for Guam because they had given our seats away. After my trying to crawl into a hole from embarrassment, we got our seats back. It is very hot here, but for one day it is very interesting. We took a bus tour and learned the history of the island. Tomorrow at 5:30 a.m., we leave for Hong Kong. I am swimming in a very warm pool this afternoon while Daddy is working on his talks in the maximum air-conditioned room. Love, The Travelers

July 20

Dear Rachel,

We got up at 4:00 this morning and got to the airport on time this time, two hours before takeoff. Had a very good flight; I saw a gigantic rainbow just before we landed here in Hong Kong. The clouds are voluminous and it is very hot. Hong Kong is fantastic, as I have told you before: Manhattan skyscrapers all around and right up to the water, a harbor full of boats and ships of different shapes and sizes. At least we are not as tired as the last time we came here, so I intend to do sightseeing to places where we have not gone before. Sorry about waking you up with our phone call; Daddy could not wait to call.

This time in Hong Kong I am trying to see the place as a "rich" tourist, for it is a tourist's paradise. We took a water tour and two bus tours and still have not seen all there is to see. The shopping is indescribable; it can't be done unless you stay up twenty-four hours a day. Even you and I could not do it justice. Unfortunately, the fun is over; we are going to Japan tomorrow for two weeks of hard work. Got some loot for you here!

July 26

Dear Rachel:

We have arrived in Fukuoka, in southern Japan, after a very good flight on a great airline, Cathay Pacific. Food galore. Now comes the hard part. I believe Daddy's crazy arrangements have us going for two weeks without stopping. I am already tired thinking about it. We keep hearing on CNN International that St. Louis is in for a hurricane! Hope not. Carry on, Doc.

July 26

Dear Rachel,

Japan is quite different from China as far as I can see at first glance. The buildings in this city are all modern and rich-looking and the streets are clean to a fault. We were picked up this morning by a fancy car and drove for one and a half hours to Kitakyushu, another southern city. We went sightseeing the rest of the day and then spent three hours in a restaurant for a real Japanese meal, complete with ten courses and two different kinds of sake (wine), one warm, one cold. I can't believe we ate all that food sitting on a cushion on the floor and are still able to walk. Anyway, tomorrow Daddy is giving a talk and I am ready to pass out right now. (The jet lag that we were so anxious to prevent by taking all those extra days has caught up with me.) The director of the hospital, who is our host, made his wife give me a unique scroll of calligraphy she had spent a year on and had gotten a prize for. I had to accept it because it is impolite not to, but the poor lady must have felt bad giving such a precious thing to a complete stranger. What could I do but thank her and tell her I would treasure the scroll always. Love, Mom

The scroll given to us by a colleague in Japan designed by his wife

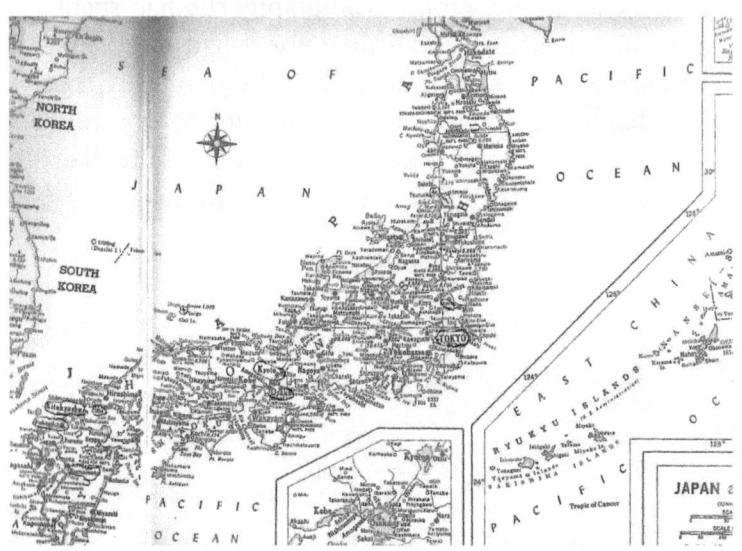

From Fukuoko to Kitakyushu to Ube, to Osaka, to Tokyo, to Hakone (north of Tokyo), to Tokyo, to Kyoto, to Kumamoto, to Fukuoko, to Tokyo in 2 weeks

July 27

Dear Rachel:

We just got taken to an art museum you would have flipped for. It had modern Japanese art, so beautiful and so esthetically pleasing that I can't even describe it to you: paintings with strong colors, delicate ceramics and screens that we have never seen before. Daddy is lecturing this afternoon and I am trying not to attend so that I can rest up. Toshi (the MD who spent three years in our lab) is waiting for us to appear in his city of Ube tomorrow morning. The scientist who is taking us around here suggested sending our luggage ahead to Tokyo, as it is impossible, in his opinion, to continue from here with eight pieces of luggage, but Daddy refuses, so we will look like the postcard I am enclosing.

The Bullet Train in Japan

One of the many gifts given to us by Toshi,
a postdoctoral fellow from Japan

A postcard from Japan indicating too many burdens

A shopping street in Ube Japan

July 28

Dear Rachel:

Toshi was overjoyed to see us, as were we to see him after two years. He took us to his house, so we were able to visit a true Japanese home. It is quite different from our homes. The furniture is simple and delicate, and there is a shrine for his ancestors with their remains in big vases in a room next to the living space; the rooms are separated by tatami-like material. Toshi's mother served us tea and delicious food she had cooked, but she did not stay with us. She is very shy and reserved and speaks only Japanese. We got to see the garden Toshi is quite proud of. Space is at a premium in Japan in general, so to have land around one's house is considered priceless.

July 30

Dear Rachel,

Just arrived in Osaka on the bullet train. It goes 280 miles an hour, and watching it go by from the outside is frightening, but once inside you don't feel that it goes that fast at all. You only have two minutes to go in and out—we just about managed it, with great ingenuity and $20 extra to the taxi driver for help to get the valises and bags up two flights of stairs! Would you believe it?—no elevators or escalators for the bullet train. The hotel is fabulous, brand-new. I want to go sightseeing this weekend, but Daddy already got three faxes and a phone call and has to give a talk soon. Anyway, I will go my own way as far as I can. Toshi sends his love to you.

July 31

Here in Osaka it is like Qumran, Israel—remember?—100 degrees and 250 percent humidity. We went to catch a sightseeing bus but missed it by a few minutes. No problem—we walked around many streets, all modern, clean, and very civilized, until we were ready to drop, then entered a department store. It was fun walking in there, but all we could afford to buy were three different kinds of pencils; everything is unbelievably expensive. Then we sat down and had tea and crumpets in there. We looked at their art—you would have liked it—then back to the hotel by bus. We lunched on raw fish and meat. Daddy ate the fish, I the meat. Tomorrow we visit with Dr. E, your favorite.

August 1

Dear Rachel:

Dr. Ema and family took us up this space-age, brand-new glass and metal tower, which dominates the city of Osaka. It is very interesting up there, what with a 360-degree view of the whole area and a movie about a spacewalk. We enjoyed the day immensely. The E. family is so sweet, and after a good lunch (no raw fish or raw meat), we returned to the fabulous air-conditioned hotel. Tomorrow I will try to venture out on my own. Daddy has to give a talk and visit an institute all day.

Tokyo Tower

Garden of a hotel near the Imperial Palace in Tokyo

August 3

Dear Rachel:

We tried calling you until 10:30 p.m. Sunday. I guess you were not home. Hope you are okay. We arrived in Tokyo on the bullet train. To our consternation, there was no escalator to go down to the street here either. Daddy looked high and low. So we had to go down three flights of stairs, one valise at a time, one bag at a time. It was pretty bad. The taxis also were far away, but now we are in a fancy hotel across from the Imperial Palace. Daddy is starving, it is 5:00 p.m., and we have had no lunch. Oh well, better listen next time, travel light.

August 5

Dear Rachel:

We walked all around the palace grounds yesterday morning. You cannot see the buildings any more than on the postcard I've enclosed, but the gardens are huge and breathtaking. Then we went to a modern art museum, which was beautiful again. Next we were picked up and I gave the talk I had rehearsed last night and early this morning on the importance of magnesium to prevent cerebral blood vessel spasms and strokes. It went okay—Daddy pointed to the slides for me, so I would not lose my place. Daddy gave his talk next, and then he went to a banquet, while I begged off and asked to go back to the hotel, as it was 9:00 p.m. Today we have the morning free then we proceed to another city.

They have their own Eiffel Tower here, the Tokyo Tower. We went up there this morning as soon as it opened. Fantastic 360-degree views, but now we have no more time to go to the Ginza (like New York's Fifth Ave.). We are being taken to Hakone to a symposium starting at 6:00 p.m. tonight. Daddy will give a talk there. He only tells me the future half a day at a time, so I won't get too angry at the schedule he has prepared. I love to look at the people here. They are so polite, bowing to each other, and so well dressed. All the women look like dolls to me. Love, the Tired (1) Travelers.

August 6

Dear Rachel,

We were taken by a private hotel car to Hakone, a two-hour ride high up in the mountains. You are supposed to be able to see Mt. Fuji from here, but it is too misty. Daddy gave a one-hour talk right after we arrived. I don't know how he does it. He only has some little crib notes and does the whole thing ad lib. After the talk there was a social hour with lots of great food and drink. Daddy is talking away, a mile a minute, to a group of people when one of the men, the one closest to him, falls on the floor. I thought for sure he had finally talked someone to death, and said so to a colleague. But the man had just fainted, it seems he had come directly from an eighteen-hour flight to the meeting and was overtired and jet-lagged. We are going back to Tokyo tomorrow.

August 7

Dear Rachel:

Just got back to Tokyo. It has been pouring and the traffic was horrendous. Therefore it took us four hours instead of two for the ride back. No sooner did we check into this gorgeous hotel than Daddy had to be interviewed by some reporters for Japanese television stations. At 6:00 p.m. we have to go to a conference. At 7:00 p.m. Daddy gives a talk. Tomorrow the same routine somewhere else. I would like to buy something, but the prices are astronomical. Love, Exhausted

Dear Rachel:

The view from the dining room of our hotel was delightful: deep green gardens, sculptured hedges and trees. Unfortunately it is now 10:00 a.m. and we are again in the bullet train, going to Kyoto. There we have another meeting tonight starting at 4:00 p.m. As you may have noted, all the meetings in this country take place toward evening. The people from Searle are taking care of us, and Daddy has finally consented to leave the two big valises in Tokyo, stored in the Otani Hotel, which will forward them to the airport the day we leave. Daddy is nervous to leave his dirty clothes, but we still have five bags and the luggage carrier to cart around. A little gentle fellow from the pharmaceutical firm is helping us cart our stuff.

August 8, Grand Kyoto Hotel

I have so much to tell you from Kyoto. After the meeting where Daddy gave a talk again, we went to a geisha house. I was the only female guest with ten men. It was a very strange experience. We ate a meal sitting on a cushion on the floor, and the geishas took care of us in a grand manner. They all were gorgeous, with lots of makeup and beautiful kimonos. Between each course, they changed into another kimono. I understand that this cost our host, the chairman of a department, a large fortune, but everybody seemed to have a grand time watching, eating, and drinking. Daddy got a special "business" card from one of the geisha girls who is supposed to be a most famous person among those girls.

Next day we went sightseeing with a scientist friend, his wife, and a superb guide. Saw the Golden Temple, the Shogun castle, a rock garden, the Temple of the Thousand Buddhas, and the biggest pagoda. Had a great Japanese lunch. Went into the bullet train to Osaka again, then to the airport and had a first-class seat in a 747 to go to Kumamoto. Here we took a forty-minute taxi ride up the mountains to a fantastic suite in the Mount Aso Hotel with views you would not believe. Searle is treating us like royalty. Tomorrow there is another meeting, Daddy gives another talk then it is good-bye Japan. There is a typhoon due here and everyone is concerned to get us out.

August 9

After a long taxi ride down the mountain to Kumamoto, Daddy gave an hour talk again. Then we were shooed into a taxi because the typhoon was too close for comfort. We took an hour trip to the Fukuoka airport. ANA airline took us to Tokyo, and after a long taxi ride, we got back to the magnificent Imperial Hotel, this time into a suite. We ordered dinner in the room, had breakfast in the morning, then the little fellow from Searle took us by taxi to Narita Airport. He stayed with us to the last minute, still gave us some presents, paid for the airport tax, and made great efforts to converse with us though his English was poor. We finally said good-bye to him, and he stayed to wave us off. The warmth of the man was extraordinary. Coming home, hope to see you soon, The Travelers

GOLDEN AMERICA

Pagoda in Japan

Inside a temple

Temple of a Thousand Buddhas in Kyoto, Japan

GOLDEN AMERICA

Our hosts Professor and Mrs. Itokawa in
front of the Golden Pavilion

Our host Professor Ytokawa, and colleagues and the Geisha girls

The number one Geisha of Kyoto

TRIPS ON BEHALF OF A BIOTECH COMPANY

Our next two trips brought us to Europe. These trips we were taking on behalf of the biotech company, which had been so very generous to us and supported a lot of our work, especially mine. We will give some talks and thus help them out by disseminating information about the new technology I had been working with to scientists and clinicians in Europe.

Returning to Europe evoked a lot of mixed feelings for me. It brought back remembrances I preferred to never think about nor talk about. But I was going with Burt, armed and protected by my blue passport, and I endeavored to push bad thoughts into the deepest corners of my memory.

Milan, Budapest, and Rome, 1997

On the evening of August 20, 1997, we were on our way to Milan. The flight was fine. We had a nice dinner, a bit of champagne, and I indulged in some crossword puzzle solving. Then I went to sleep for several hours, something I had never been able to do on a plane. At 7:00 a.m., we were presented with breakfast—a roll, butter and jam, coffee—and arrived in Milan, not at all exhausted as we usually were after a long flight. We took a taxi for about $100 and arrived at the Hotel Principe di Savoia, to a lovely, old-fashioned, comfortable room and an all-marble bathroom. The furniture in the room was made of dark and light brown wood inlay, polished and glistening, and the easy chairs and sofa were upholstered in royal-blue velvet. To our pleasant surprise, we were allowed into the room immediately, a rare treat, since in Europe there is usually a long wait when arriving in the morning before one can occupy a room.

I visited the pool, letting the warm water embrace me. I was alone at that early hour. I did my forty laps, took a shower, and stretched out in the solarium with its 180-degree view around a well built-up city. The sun was pleasantly warm, and a slow breeze waved some tall potted plants lazily back and forth.

I returned to the room, and we asked the concierge to direct us to a restaurant within walking distance. He warned us that most restaurants and stores were closed in August because the natives are on vacation at the seashore. He recommended a pizzeria where we had our favorite Italian fare: we shared one pizza, a plate of spaghetti *pomodoro* (tomato sauce), one *insalata mista* (mixed green salad), and each had a glass of white wine, one lemon sorbet, and a cup of cappuccino. We walked back to the hotel for several hours of deep sleep. Around 4:00 a.m., I woke up; and no matter how many sheep I counted, I could not go back to sleep while Burt was happily snoozing away. Jet lag had caught up with me. Too bad we had ordered an early breakfast and seats on a sightseeing bus. By 8:00 a.m., I was dead tired and out of sorts despite our favorite rolls, butter and jam, and two cups of strong coffee.

Cathedral in Milan, Italy

The bus took us to Piazza del Duomo. The cathedral was a most beautiful sight: a huge, lacy, light-brown masterpiece with thin spires reaching up, beset with statues and gargoyles—simply magnificent, the laciness of the walls giving it an airy, light feeling despite its massive size. The doors were replete with carving. We entered the cathedral with its beautiful stained-glass windows and huge columns. The windows dominated, and each one, when looked at from left to right, their panels depicted a Bible story. The rich colors were created from metals baked into the glass, like copper and manganese; the church took five hundred years to be constructed. A little hole allows a sunray to come in and light up the zodiac-decorated floor exactly at 12 noon. It was hard to leave this treasure, but the tour had to proceed.

We walked across to the Galleria Vittorio Emanuele, a glass-roofed place of shops and restaurants in the shape of a big cross—the very first mall, an impressive, marble-floored, high-domed structure. We then got to the piazza where the famous La Scala opera house was located. It was disappointing. We expected a grand sight from its reputation, but instead, it was a somewhat neglected-looking yellow building. We walked up seven flights of stairs to see the red velvet box seats and the orchestra seats below; a huge chandelier was on the floor for cleaning and repair. The little museum, Della Scala, was impressive with pictures of Verdi, Puccini, Maria Callas, and many other great singers, a spinet used by Mozart, and locks of hair from composers safely kept in a special cabinet. Next, the bus took us to see *The Last Supper* by Leonardo, which hangs in a rectory of the Santa Maria delle Grazie church. We passed the Sforza Castle, the business district streets, where the haute couture shops were located (though their doors were all closed), and finally back to our hotel. There, Burt rested and I swam and sunned. We went back to the Galleria to have our usual delicious lunch then returned to the cathedral to linger in its beauty and take it all in at our leisure.

On Saturday, we went to attend services at the Temple Centrale, an edifice with gold and blue writings and gold decorations on the doorway. I had very mixed feelings of what I encountered there—glad to see what looked like a newly flourishing Jewish community again but amazed that any Jewish person would want to return to a place that had persecuted them. Inside was a marble ark and rows of newly upholstered colorful seats, multicolored Hebrew letters on wide windows, and menorah pictures on the walls. From the ark were taken small Torah scrolls decorated with silver plates and crowns. The service was fast and somewhat unfamiliar as it was Sephardic (a service derived from the Jews of Spain). No one approached us, as if afraid to intrude (I remembered my parents bringing home strangers for Shabbat meals many times, so very long ago). In the afternoon, we toured a modern-art museum and the Brera museum with its many paintings of saints and some impressionist works. The next evening, we proceeded to Budapest.

At the airport, we were taken by bus to a faraway Malév Airlines plane. We had to go up many stairs to reach its entrance. We got a delicious Hungarian dinner on the one-and-a-half-hour flight. We arrived in Budapest and were met by Dr. Maria C., our hostess, who greeted us with a bouquet of flowers. She and a manager from the biotech company put us in a taxi, and we arrived at the Marriott where we were given a suite of rooms: a living room, dressing room, bedroom, a balcony with a magnificent view of the palace and lit-up bridges, Fisherman's

Bastion visible in the light, the Danube flowing in between. What a view! Budapest is just a beautiful city by night and by day. Its nickname is Paris of the East, which does it justice. We slept for five hours and then I read a book about Budapest we had received from Maria, and admired the spectacular view, the king's castle, indirectly illuminated, and the bridges a necklace of lights. The next day was a meeting in our hotel. Burt gave a great presentation of our work. I followed with my own talk. Maria gave a follow-up presentation, and then we all went to a lovely lunch in the hotel.

View in Budapest, Hungary

Later, we walked by ourselves, past graceful buildings along the Danube to the technical university across the bridge. We saw some churches that were being renovated, then came upon an impressive building with ceramic tiles on the walls, two turrets reaching up to the sky, and clocks in the windows. Burt claimed he recognized this building from a book as being a synagogue, but I did not believe him until I saw a Star of David on the gates of a fence around the façade. It too was being renovated. In the back, there was a smaller building with a rounded roof, and several men wearing yarmulkes and some ladies with little white lace hats were waiting to enter. It was one of the highlights of my day. Here was a Jewish temple, being renovated and revitalized after the terrible devastation of the Holocaust. Did I dare believe that Europe was accepting the Jewish population this time for good? Sadly, I could not believe that, and I could not understand the people settling in a place that had been so hostile to them.

Next day, we went to another conference location to register, and we talked with some scientists from the States about the effect of noise on the physiology of the human body. We inquired about some tours, but our feet took us back to the temple we had seen from the outside. It was open, and we could not get over the size, the beauty of the ark, all in marble. The ladies had their seats two floors up. There were rows and rows of carved wooden seats, two golden stairs leading to two elevated golden recesses for the rabbi or anyone else to give their sermon. We visited the synagogue's museum with its silver treasures, then exited to a little cemetery and saw a tree made of a silver trunk and long silver branches with their leaves each commemorating a member of the temple who had succumbed in the Holocaust. We purchased some items to help support the temple: a cream-colored crocheted lady's cap with royal-blue velvet trim, a mezuzah Burt liked, a small set of candlesticks, and a picture book of the temple. We returned happy, and Burt prepared a brand-new talk for the next morning. It is still a wonder to me, after all these years, how he does it.

The following morning, we took a cab to the university and found a large auditorium with about three thousand people—engineers and scientists interested in the reduction of noise in the environment. There were several exhibitions showing materials for noise reduction to be used in industry on airplanes and in car construction, and some noise-measurement devices. We listened to talks on the effect of noise stress on the body, especially the ear, hearing loss being a prominent result. Then Burt gave his talk and, to my surprise, did a good job sticking to the topic and staying within his allotted time. He talked about the deleterious effect repeated loud noises have on the heart. We then had a delicious lunch in the Hotel Gellért, Hungarian goulash, *nockerl* (a side dish made of little pieces of boiled dough), and *palachinta* (delicate pancakes filled with fruit) with a colleague friend and his wife, who had invited us to the meeting. We exchanged pleasantries, bragged about our children, talked about the science of the morning, and promised to keep in touch. Then we relaxed back at the hotel, walked a bit, and made some small purchases of the typical embroidery of the region where both sides of the material are patterned equally so you can use it on either side.

Next day, we went sightseeing with Maria and a private guide in a small bus. We visited the castle, with its many bejeweled remnants of the monarchy, and Fisherman's Bastion, which featured a statue of King Stephan, the founder of Hungary, riding proudly on a horse. We heard of the many invasions, destructions, and reconstructions that occurred over the years. We proceeded to a little village, a tourist attraction with many quaint shops and old coffeehouses. We stopped for coffee and bought a mysterious box of many-colored woods that we could not get open, no matter how we tried. We thought it would be a secret forever. (Rachel opened it in five minutes when we gave it to her, but that was a fluke, we said, kidding her.)

Szeged Sygagogue indoors

Szeged Synagogue

On the following morning, we were picked up by two representatives of Nova Biomedical (the company that had designed the electrode vital to our work), kind young men who took us for three hours in an air-conditioned car through the heat and humidity to Szeged. We went to see the scientific exhibits some minutes away from our new hotel, then walked back and visited the Szeged Synagogue, one of the largest and most beautiful temples of Europe; indeed, it was breathtaking both inside and out. We returned to the hotel, were picked up for a cheese and wine party, then invited to a dinner of fish soup, a famous Hungarian dish that was less than palatable to our unaccustomed taste buds. The wine flowed, and Burt still had to prepare a new talk, which was scheduled for the next morning at 8:20 a.m. He managed to stay up most of the night, got up to have breakfast after a couple of hours of sleep, and we went to the meeting. The audience turned out to be three people. I was rather upset, but our hostess said to wait, that people in Hungary tend to come late in the morning. After forty-five minutes of anxious waiting on my part and Burt's pacing around the hall, we did have a goodly audience, which further grew as he gave his talk, another masterful job. We talked a bit to some of the scientists, then were taken on a small sightseeing tour: some old churches, a rather grandiose-looking Turkish bath left from the Turkish Empire, an award-winning art deco building with tulip designs, a music-playing and figure-moving clock, a square devoted to busts of famous people who were from Szeged or who had spent time there—like Liszt and Albert Szent-Györgyi, the Szent-Györgyi Medical University, and a fine-looking opera house.

We left our guide and driver at the railroad station and took a two-and-a-half-hour train ride back to Budapest, though the driver offered to take us. It was a more relaxing ride as the driver could not speak a word of English, and it would have been very awkward. Back in our hotel in Budapest, we passed out from tiredness, and then I made the mistake of insisting that we save our taxi money and instead take the tram to the Gellért for dinner. No sooner did we get into the tram than the two of us were surrounded and crowded in by a group of Gypsies, separated from each other, and unable to move. At the next station, the Gypsies left, and I saw that my pocketbook had been unzipped, though I had not felt a thing and was holding on to it tight. My wallet was gone. Burt had always prided himself on the fact that his wallet was squeezed so tightly in his back pocket that no one could have forced it out. However, he discovered that his front pocket was empty of his money holder, and he had not felt a thing either. For the price of a $5 taxi, we lost over $300. Burt got angry with me, which was well-deserved—it was not my finest hour—but we still calmed down enough to order dinner, and though we could not talk about anything else but the professional craft of the Gypsies, the good food soothed us.

We carefully walked back to the hotel, having no cash for the cab, looking around furtively and holding on to each other. We slept fitfully and had to rise at 6:00 the next morning to take a flight to Rome. We managed to catch the plane on empty stomachs. I fell on the escalator but did not really get hurt, and we obtained nice big seats on the plane and rolls and coffee, for which we were grateful.

We arrived in Rome and were delivered by a taxi to the Grand Hotel, next to the watchful statue of Moses pointing to the people below. We had the usual wait to get to our room as it was morning, so we walked around and found a place to have our favorite Italian fare: spaghetti *pomodoro, insalata mista,* and gelato. Then we took possession of our room, changed out of the clothes we had been wearing for three days, and walked past some of the glory of Rome—many churches, ruins, columns, obelisks, amphitheaters, the Victor Emmanuel monument—and found our way to the major synagogue of Rome. It stood there majestic, lone among the hundreds of churches, and was being protected by carabinieri (soldiers) on all sides. It was closed for sightseers, and we hoped to return.

Trevi Fountain in Rome

The next day, we went to the temple by cab but were reluctant to tell the driver to let us off there (since anti-Semitism in Europe is, after all, ever-present), so we asked him to take us to the Victor Emmanuel monument and wandered to the temple by way of the former ghetto's narrow streets paved with cobblestones. The temple is sumptuous—double columns, great menorahs all around, much marble, and a cupola decorated in a leaf motif. The women's section was separated by a trellis. During the services, the acoustics left a lot to be desired, but the prayer book was easy to follow. The women, much to my surprise, mostly talked among themselves; only a few prayed at all. When it was over, we walked back to the hotel and had lunch at a nice outdoor restaurant nearby, enjoying our usual fare. We never get tired of the taste of that food, and it cannot be duplicated at home or in any Italian restaurant in the States. In the afternoon, we took a bus tour and saw Michelangelo's Moses, some fine churches inside and out, the Forum, the Circus Maximus, and the Colosseum, the Spanish Steps and the Trevi Fountain. In the evening, we had dinner at a pizzeria where a man was selling flowers. I wanted to get one but had no change to give him and felt bad; he seemed so desolate. Burt reached into his pocket and gave him an American dollar, and I got a beautiful set of violets with a grateful smile. We slept until 2:00 a.m. then heard the news bulletin of Princess Diana's fatal accident, a crack-up of her car pursued by paparazzi. We stayed up after that, listening to CNN Continental's reporting. Next morning, we had an early flight, had a quick breakfast, and left for home, rather weary of the trip.

Rome-Athens-Crete
September 29, 1997

On our second trip for the biotech company, we first went from Newark to Rome and stayed in Rome for two days to get over the jet lag.

The next day it was off to Athens. We saw typical Mediterranean white houses with terraces, after passing rocky white hills with little vegetation. They reminded me of Israel, all those rocky hills. The houses were similar to the houses in Portugal, replete with green-leafed plants and flowers in full bloom on every balcony. Dr. T, our host, picked us up and brought us to a wonderful Hilton hotel with a lovely room, complete with a terrace looking out to the Acropolis. That same evening, we had to go to temple as it was the beginning of the High Holidays, and we had corresponded with the congregation to say that we were going to be there for the New Year. The temple was situated in a poor-looking, broken-up street in the old part of town; the taxi driver had trouble understanding what we wanted, though we had a map, but the Hilton doorman helped out. At the entrance from the street where the synagogue was located, there was a barricade of cars and people checking passports. On the roof of the synagogue were men with rifles.

As we were let into a rather stark-looking building, the president of the temple came over to us, welcomed us, and told us the rabbi would give us all our meals. We were embarrassed by this kindness and respectfully declined, saying we had made arrangements already. This was a rather painful situation as the rabbi had prepared extra meals for us for the two days of the holiday. No matter how much we excused ourselves, we could see the hurt on the man's face, not a good way to start the New Year. Well, we spent the next two mornings in the synagogue; the service was very dignified, but the women, separated from the men in an upstairs balcony, spent the time talking to each other as was the case in Rome. It was not too crowded up there, and there were plenty of prayer books, so I was comfortable and able to follow the service, even if the melodies of the prayers were foreign. Burt had brought his own prayer book, borrowed from our synagogue at home.

The Acropolis in Athens

We did no sightseeing in Athens for those two days. The next morning, it was time to go to Crete, where the meeting was held. The evening before leaving for Crete, we were invited by Dr. T, along with a colleague from Japan, to a typical fish restaurant in which you chose your own fresh fish from an iced counter. The fish was the best, freshest fish ever; it melted in your mouth as you ate it. There were also some hot and cold appetizers, chickpeas and fried eggplant, all most delicate and delicious. Next morning, we were picked up by Dr. T's husband and taken to the airport to fly to Crete.

In Crete, the sun was shining all the time, the sky was blue, the water blue-green, calm and warm, and we could see another small island on the horizon. But it was five long days of meetings, and I attended every minute, and so did Burt, so there was no sightseeing at all. All I did for relaxation was to swim in the saltwater pool of the hotel at lunchtime. We did have one evening of socializing with plenty of delicious food and free-flowing good wine. There was roast pig—which our table partners kept praising, but we were not tempted to taste—roast chicken, roast lamb, hamburgers, and assorted vegetables and salads. There was a dessert cart loaded with so many goodies that Burt finally forbade me to take one more morsel of food.

The science at the meeting was good, especially new lipid studies I was thrilled about. I stuck my neck out several times to criticize some work done with an instrument I had found to be wanting in accuracy and discussed results of a study done by Swedish and Australian investigators, who agreed with my results. On the last day, the meeting went until 8:15 p.m.; we then had to pack and catch a plane to Athens. It was a terrible rush, what with Burt's hundreds of slides all over the room and background papers galore, which he had studied before each session. We finally went to gobble down some of the good food left over from the social night, and I could not leave before I consumed two helpings of a combination of ice cream, Jell-O, and cake while Burt was busy talking to a colleague and not watching me. At the airport, there were some trinkets to be had for souvenirs, but I was simply too worn out and could not choose.

We arrived in Athens very late, but there was Dr. T's husband to pick us up and bring us to the Hilton nevertheless. The next morning, we slept until 9:00 and got breakfast at the concierge level, a special room done up beautifully for special guests of the hotel. We then took a taxi to the Acropolis as it had beckoned us to visit the two previous days in Athens. It was way up on a hill, with strong walls all around.

There were three structures: the entrance to the Acropolis, with six columns on each side; the Palateum, a temple to Athena with many columns, quite intact, being kept up by the Greek authority so it would not become more damaged, but also not to be restored by any additions beyond what had been done in the 1950s; and the Erechtheum, a temple to Athena and Poseidon with thirteen statues standing and holding up the roof columns. There was a museum featuring large statues from buildings that had been destroyed ages ago. We were so satisfied to have been able to visit this interesting place that our spirits rallied from having missed all there was to see in Crete, which some of the other scientists had been talking about. On our way down the Acropolis, we had to walk, the traffic being as horrendous in Athens as it is in Rome. Taxis have to be begged to stop; they will only take you if you are going in the same direction as other passengers that are already crammed in the cab. To our amazement, on our way to the hotel, we saw a building marked "State University of New York" in big letters. It is an exchange college, we found out from a brochure with pictures of New York and SUNY New Paltz.

After a short while of waiting in the Hilton, Dr. T took us to the airport, and we left Greece to go back to Rome.

In Rome, we barely had time to reach the Excelsior Hotel because the streets were overcrowded on account of soccer matches taking place there at this time of the year, and there was also a multitude of police present to try and prevent the riots that had taken place previously among the players. It was sundown, and the beginning of Yom Kippur. We had no time to eat dinner, and thus had to subsist on the lunch we had consumed on Alitalia, which had been very good. I said my prayers that evening from the book Burt had brought along. The memorial candles I had brought and lit, which are supposed to last all night and next day, were extinguished next morning, which made me upset for they were lit in memory of both our parents. Yom Kippur day, when we fasted, was hard from beginning to end, although we did not get sick or very hungry despite the fact we had not eaten any supper the night before. The big temple was very crowded, and there was no prayer book to be had for me. Two women, whom I asked about it, told me harshly to go buy my own the next day. The chanting was totally foreign to us. This congregation, evidently, claims to be the direct descendants of members of the old temple in Jerusalem. I finally found an everyday prayer book and had to make do with that. I said what I could, but I was upset that I could not figure out from the chanting when the congregation was saying the prayers for remembrance of the departed, an important part of this particular holiday. When I asked some ladies about that, they did not know what I was talking about. In fact, none of the women were praying; they were simply constantly talking to each other. All the women, however, were quiet for one thing, the benediction by the Cohen (descendant of the original high priest), who did this three times during the day. The women, at that moment, crowded together, turned around toward the door, covered each other's heads with their hands as if in blessing, and were quiet until it was over. I had never witnessed such a thing.

When the last part of the service began, the whole gigantic temple filled up; there was no standing room left. I barely could breathe and had to hold on to my seat with both hands. Finally, the shofar (ram's horn) was sounded, and seconds later, absolutely the whole crowd headed for the door. It was real mayhem, and for the next thirty minutes, I could not find Burt, who had been in the men's section. I got rather frantic thinking that perhaps he had gotten ill, and who knows what had happened since he did not speak a word of Italian. I stationed myself at the entrance of the men's section and later found that he had stationed himself at the entrance of the women's section and frantically waited for me. I finally unburdened myself to a security agent and asked him if someone had gotten ill, and he said only a young boy did, and I should calm down and just wait where I was. Burt finally appeared, a little put out, but I was so happy to see him among that huge crowd. The crowd slowly thinned out a little, but many of the people had brought canteens of coffee and food packages and were now enjoying them. No one offered us anything, and Burt was starting to feel faint. It was impossible to get a taxi, so a soldier who had noticed us offered Burt and me some of his mineral water and saved the day. A family nearby, when they saw the carabiniere offer us both water, gave us some breadsticks, which were very welcome. We thanked them all and wished them well, the family and the soldier, and walked slowly back to our hotel as we had walked to the temple in the morning. On the way, we stopped to have our favorite spaghetti, etc., which we ate a bit too fast. Fixed up with a Tums each, we went to sleep to get up early next morning, rush down a breakfast, and catch the plane for home with the realization that I would have to teach the very next day, kind of unprepared and terribly jet lagged. I made a transparency of a picture of the Acropolis to show the students before the lecture, in order to break the ice.

THE UNEXPECTED GIFT OF GRANDCHILDREN

While I never had a mom to talk to me about dating and marriage, I would never have dated someone out of my faith for any length of time, and I certainly would not have married someone out of my faith. This would have been unthinkable to me. I was convinced, somehow, that I had passed this certainty of belief over to my daughter just as it had come to me instinctively, and that it would not be necessary to talk about it to Rachel. Burt had related to me that his father often said to him, "If you bring a non-Jew into this house to marry, I will break both of your legs." This made me laugh and seemed quite extreme and unnecessary to me. I was sure that all such important things are passed to your children by example and DNA, resulting in a strong instinct as to what is the right thing to do. Marriage between people of different faiths is too difficult, in most cases, to make it work, especially for any children that come along; it would give them hardships and mixed feelings growing up that are burdens added to normal growing pains. Anyways, that was both our opinions.

During Rachel's college career, she had dated an Orthodox boy and some other Jewish boys, which made us not worry about anything untoward coming around the corner. It turned out that when Rachel finally introduced us to a young man she was serious about, he had been born to another faith but was studying to convert to Judaism and was seriously engaged in learning all about the religion. He seemed a nice person and, in all respects, good to Rachel. Michael had a PhD in biochemistry and was a whiz with computers; he had worked in a lab near Rachel's in Memphis. Soon after, she became engaged, and we planned the wedding.

Rachel and Michael got married in a small synagogue in Jersey City where we had moved to. Three Rabbis attended the ceremony: the Rabbi from the Jersey synagogue, the Rabbi from the Whitestone temple we had attended before, and her favorite Rabbi, who had taught her for her bat mitzvah (Jewish confirmation). Her bridesmaids were friends of hers from Brandeis. Our former PhD student's daughter and one of Michael's nieces were two little flower-girls. The guests were Michael's four sisters and parents, all the people who had worked with us and for us that were still in the United States, my friend Helen and husband, my friend Margot and husband, my friend Marjorie and her sisters, my cousin Ida, Burt's favorite aunt, cousins, friends from various schools, and Rachel's two favorite teachers from high school. It was a fine June wedding complete with music, dancing, toasts, and speeches.

Rachel and Michael, Panda—the dog, and Michael's elderly cat moved to the Midwest, where they both did research together in the same lab while Rachel also worked in a hospital several months of the year.

For my first birthday after Michael became part of the family, he wrote an essay about becoming Jewish and framed it within a blue Star of David. It said something like this: "Judaism is optimistic, rational, practical, conservative, ethical, and moral; it honors learning, it is humane, it is based on the premise that one was intended to enjoy life, it is eternal and gives evidence that theism becomes believable." It is entitled "Why I Want to Be a Jew." I have treasured this gift and displayed it for everyone to see. Michael has kept up with the religion, following it faithfully. I respect and am friendly with his whole family, especially his mom and dad.

I can't forget to mention the masterful present Michael made for Burt after several years of being in the family. Michael made a photograph the size of a mural, on which he showed the titles and beginnings of many of our published papers intermingled by photographs of members of our family in chronological order and photographs of places we had been to. It is now hanging at the entrance of our home, taking up an entire wall, and everyone visiting us cannot get over the artistry and cleverness.

After two years of marriage, Rachel announced that she was going to have a baby and asked if I would come and help. Having grandchildren had never entered my mind, so I was very excited at the prospect, and took a leave of absence from my position after the baby was born and moved into the proud new parents' house. It was a labor of love taking care of little Rebecca, and I immediately grew attached to her as I had to Rachel before. I gladly took care of the house and prepared dinner and shopped, and there was this sweet little being who took over my heart. Burt, in the meantime, had to fend for himself. He came to visit for a few days every month, and we spoke over the phone several times a day.

After about ten months of this arrangement, Burt started feeling pains in his chest, and it became imperative I move back home. It was hard leaving the baby, who had taken me over with every fiber of her being, and Rachel became hysterical, not trusting anyone else, though we quickly looked for a suitable babysitter. It was a very painful separation for me, and Rachel did not help the situation by accusing me of abandoning her when she needed me most. But Burt needed me more, and he had to come first and foremost. After two months with the babysitter, Rachel placed Rebecca in a well-recommended day-care program at the Jewish Community Center, which helped Rachel feel more relaxed and secure and in which Rebecca thrived.

Back home, I took care of Burt and went back to work as if I had never left. As Burt's heart problem subsided with the aid of proper medication and bed rest, he became himself again and was able to work normally. We eventually started visiting Rachel and her family once a month and enjoying the grandchild.

RETIREMENT

Several years after returning to New York, having worked for forty years by then and being asked to do an enormous amount of teaching and to direct two courses by a new chairman (which left much less time for my research and yet gave me no permanent position nor more remuneration), I decided to retire from my job and start a new life for myself, enjoying the freedom from the daily subway rides. I still would actively help Burt in planning and writing the various projects he was engaged in and give a few lectures to the physician's assistants and physical therapy students once a year—because Burt tended to make the material too difficult and detailed for those particular students.

I promptly enrolled in a writing course I had been dreaming about and walked city blocks like Fifth Avenue and Madison Avenue, feeling like a lady and enjoying the freedom and leisure. It was fun and felt like an expansion of my horizons. I loved my writing class and was eager to continue after the first term, but it was not to be because Rachel informed me that she was going to have another baby and asked me to please come to help her out again. I, of course, said yes, sure, but since I was now older and Rachel had moved to a bigger house in a totally residential area far away from a supermarket (I had never learned to drive a car, and there were no subways or buses available), I could not see myself taking care of a new baby, a three-year-old young lady, a big dog, a big house, and shopping for and cooking dinners. So I looked for and found a place nearby where I could take care of the baby and the granddaughter sometimes as a bonus. The baby turned out to be a sweet boy, a cute little thing whom I loved dearly from the first day I saw him and who loved me back as Rebecca had done.

I took care of David at my place. He was an easy child and a pleasure to hold and cuddle and walk outdoors and feed and do all the things that needed doing, and he gave me time to read and write while he had his naps. Every evening, his mom or dad picked him up to take him home, which allowed me some very much appreciated leisure time. As usual, his grandpa came to visit one weekend a month, and he came to play with and enjoy his two grandkids as I did. They were the apples of our eyes, precious beings we had never even dreamed about.

As David grew bigger, I discovered something I had never come across before: while he adored his sister and followed her around wherever she went, once he could crawl, she at times rejected him and wanted nothing to do with him. As Rachel and I had been only children, sibling rivalry was not something I was familiar with, nor did I forgive it. Here was this sweet child and another sweet child who could turn nasty. While it hurt me to witness this happening, I thanked God for having had just one offspring so I did not have to deal with this strange hostility. (My friend Judy, who had talked me into having Rachel, had four more children, but she and her family had emigrated to Israel right after obtaining her PhD, so her influence was too long-distance!)

After David's first birthday Rachel told me she wanted to put him into the day-care center his sister was enrolled in, although this time I wanted to stay longer since I was retired, Burt was managing better, and I was very attached to the little boy. But Rachel insisted. Doubtless, she wanted to make the transition easier to handle and prevent any sudden emergencies. So I moved back to New York and worried about the kids.

LE CHÂTEAU

We visited the grandchildren as often as we could while I made a new life for myself, reading, writing, and getting used to a new area. We had finally bought a house after living in apartments that inevitably became crammed full of Burt's possessions. We had been looking for a home for close to fifteen years—it had become like a hobby of ours—but we could never find what satisfied both of us. It was usually too small for Burt or too big for me (I feared becoming a slave to the thing), or much too expensive for our pocketbook. We finally found what pleased us both. It possessed plenty of space for our family to come visit: a family room, living, dining and three bedrooms on the first floor, and, my pride and joy, a little office of my own, and a single enormous room for Burt on the second floor. It was a dream come true for Burt, who liked lots of space and had fantasized of owning a genuine library all his own, complete with bookcases filled with his innumerable books and papers and space for his wealth of CDs.

Burt had been buying books that interested him, like sets of classical writers, since he was a boy. He had kept all the textbooks he had accumulated from school and never parted with them. In addition, he bought other texts to teach himself new material and help him write the many papers he published. And he had favorite mystery and historical writers, whose works he could not pass up.

    He was happy as a lark up there in his room, and his writing of papers increased exponentially. He was finally able to extract data from the deep freeze, data from work that had been done years ago but, of course, was as fresh in his mind as if it had been produced yesterday. As for me, it took me a long time to believe I was part-owner of this castle. All the beautiful presents we had received from all over the world suddenly could be displayed: the Japanese scrolls could be hung in full splendor, the prints we had purchased in museums could grace the walls, and the precious pieces of pottery from China and different parts of Europe could be displayed in glass cabinets bought for that purpose. We called our house Le Château, and I proudly hung a big American flag near the front door to remember always where I had come from and where I now was. I always wore my love for this country close to my heart.

DAVID

When David first started to talk, he sounded as cute as a button, to use a cliché. He made two- or three-word sentences that were music to my ears, and I repeated them to Burt, or he to me. Soon, however, difficulties started to arise: he started to stutter. He was conscious of this difficulty. At one point, he asked his grandpa, "When will I be able to speak like other people?" It broke my heart. When he started school, he had difficulties reading. This put me in agony. I was convinced that my gene pool had been mutated due to all the stress I had suffered for so long, and I had passed a defect to my grandchild. His difficulties in school persisted, and all I could do was love him more while his sister compounded the problem sometimes by telling her brother he was doing things wrong. This made it even harder for David. I mourned the possibility that I had indeed passed some horrible gene along and even sometimes wished I had not had our daughter, who had given us such a lot of pleasure, but now was the reason an innocent little boy had difficulties, and I was clueless how to help him. Rachel refused to talk to me about it. David was such a loving and giving child, he was uniquely solicitous and caring about others and would give the shirt off his back to his sister or his friends. It was not fair; life was not fair. So far, he had friends, and his teachers seemed to be good to him, but his parents were not giving him the kind of understanding I was wishing and praying for.

The children were such a bittersweet presence. We loved them so dearly but worried about them so much. Rebecca seemed to manage, but I could not console myself over the boy. He was on my mind so very often. There had grown a wall between Rachel and me; I could not say anything without her getting unreasonably angry, and we then would not talk for weeks on end. We grew apart, and it became impossible for me to reason with her or beg her to ease David's difficulties with understanding and proper care. I simply could not approach her anymore. I reproached myself for my cowardice, but what could I do if she refused to listen? She told me to mind my own business and that these were her children, and she would deal with them as she saw fit. After many fights, I gave up and stayed quiet. I suffered in silence, except to overburden Burt with my worries whenever it got too much for me. And after a while, I managed to compartmentalize my worries so that, at times, I forgot and lived on as if all was okay.

LIFE GOES ON
MARCH 10, 2005

We are supposed to go to Washington to speak to some people in Congress about the work we are doing, but Burt has had some chest discomfort for several evenings in a row, and I insist he go to his internist first. The doctor sees a bad EKG and sends us immediately to a cardiologist, who admits Burt to the hospital the same day, March 8, 2005. Burt insists on a private room so I can stay with him, and threatens the admitting person that he will go home unless he gets a room with a cot for me. We wait several hours, but he gets his way. Burt is hooked up to a saline and heparin drip overnight and, next morning, is taken to the cardiac lab for an angiogram. I sit and wait for three hours in acute agony. Then the doctor calls the nurses' station and wants to speak to me. He tells me that Burt does not want to have bypass surgery (one option for his condition), so instead, he can put a new type of stent into one of his coronary arteries. Is that okay with me? I am shocked that the procedure has to be done right away, but I cannot say no since that is what Burt wants. After two hours, during which I can't find a spot for myself, pacing and sitting, numb and mindless, I sit on my eyeglasses and break the frame.

Finally, I can go to see Burt. He is lying in the recovery room with four other patients. He is conscious and seems not too bad but only complains about being cold. I thank God fervently and get some more covers for him, and forty minutes later, he is taken to a cubicle where there are other patients, each hooked up to an EKG, and nurses nearby to monitor and supervise. After a short while, Burt asks to go to his own room; he is not comfortable and cannot rest or sleep in this arrangement. The nurse refuses, but Burt gets very angry. The nurse, seeing his agitation, reluctantly gives in and lets him go to the room we share. He calms down and soon is offered some dinner: vegetables, a small piece of grilled chicken, and pudding, all very healthy food. I take note of the food and vow to cook only this way.

Burt sleeps well after that, and the next morning, we are hoping to go home. One nurse says we should wait until the doctor comes in, around 1:00 p.m. Another nurse tells us we can leave but should first pass by the doctor's office. She unhooks him from the EKG and helps him dress. When we arrive at the doctor's office, he takes one look at Burt and starts to yell for him to go back to his room and yells at the nurses over the phone. We go back to the room and wait for him to come by. He does come by at around 1:00 p.m., examines Burt, and says it is okay to go home provided Burt takes it real easy, does nothing but walk around for thirty minutes a day in the house, and comes back for an appointment in two weeks. We take a taxi home, and Burt has a long, restoring sleep.

Next morning, I go to the lab to pick up mail, make a phone call to excuse us for not coming to Washington, read e-mail, and save some samples someone has refrigerated for me to analyze, which have come from St. Jude Children's Research Hospital. I return home and we take it easy again. Saturday, I get the newspapers for Burt to read, and rest again, except Burt slips in the kitchen and collapses on his backside, to my horror, but he gets up and says he is okay. He lies down and takes a nap, and I worry myself sick all over again.

After several weeks of taking it easy and a satisfying examination by his cardiologist, Burt was allowed to return to work. He continues to work, exercises on his stationary bike thirty minutes a day, and we subsist on grilled fish, grilled or baked chicken, or turkey with lots of vegetables and fruit on the side. We travel only occasionally to see the grandkids. The meetings are a thing of the past.

MY FAMILY

More years have passed, and the grandchildren have been growing. Rebecca, now fourteen, has been going to a Jewish day school and can read Hebrew flawlessly, even without the presence of vowels (something I never mastered). She can do a whole service in the temple, and she can read the Torah. She is a budding artist, having learned to paint in various media, and I was able to extricate one of her paintings, with great difficulty and over her mother's objection, to take home to our house. She plays the piano fairly well and sings in a choir, having a very pleasant voice inherited from her dad. She has written some essays for statewide contests and received several awards for them. She has done charity work by donating her long hair to children who had treatments and lost theirs. She has taken part in activities to collect money for the Diabetes Foundation and cancer research, and she has made friends with one of her mother's patients and is in the process of illustrating a book with her of the latter's experiences.

David, now eleven, is no longer stuttering much and is a fine athlete. He has gotten several awards in statewide gymnastics contests. He loves to ski in the winter and swim in the summer. He is learning to play baseball in the spring, to the great satisfaction of his grandpa. His favorite subjects in school are science, social studies, and math. He is a Cub Scout and into robotics, and his group has won some contests even in that. He plays the saxophone and the xylophone and sings in a little choir. He is the most humble, polite, and caring individual of the family.

I have to admit to myself and their parents that despite my great worries, they did things right.

Our daughter is working hard and is good to her little patients, each of whom she befriends, and the parents seem to think the world of her. I have seen a video of a father thanking her for her astute diagnosis of his child's difficult case, made for the Hospital she works in. She has done well in the lab and made several important discoveries, but she constantly worries about getting grants, the usual bane of a scientist in the present era. We finally have made peace with each other.

Our son-in-law runs the lab full-time, cooks, shops, and picks up the kids from their various activities, besides running the Cub Scout group and helping with the robotics group. As for me, I will interrupt him anytime from his endeavors when I have a problem using my computer. It is so much easier to ask him a question, which he always can answer, than to look it up in the *Computer for Dummies* book he has given me for my birthday.

So all in all, we can be proud of our family, and we are looking forward to each visit with them.

GOLDEN AMERICA

Obtaining my citizenship papers was my proudest achievement early on, after coming to America. Five years after my eighteenth birthday, I was privileged to obtain what I thought would be an unattainable and even unimaginable status, that of being accepted as a citizen with full rights of staying in this country, moving about freely, having a real, valid passport, and, wonder of wonders, voting in elections. Each time I voted, it was a new joy, a feeling of new pride, feelings I never lost throughout the years. These gifts I was able to comprehend to be mine slowly, even in the bad years. Although I was shy about wearing a Star of David or openly discussing my religion, I was accepted as a full member of society. I was an American citizen with unalienable rights to life, liberty, and the pursuit of happiness.

I took voting seriously, but it was more like a privilege than a choice I had to make for I saw goodness in everyone. I proudly voted for President Eisenhower to be president a second term, he who had helped to liberate the world from devastation and thus had liberated me personally to live in this great land I loved with all my heart and soul.

I also voted for President Kennedy, who was able to avoid a nuclear war and start the first steps to put a man on the moon. I enjoyed watching his family antics and rejoiced in the era of Camelot. But sadly, as everyone else, I remember vividly where I was and what I was doing when the news came of the dastardly deed that took him from us. We had Johnson then, and the magic of Camelot was gone. I voted for President Nixon and admired his good works with China. After meeting and then marrying Burt, who was an avid reader of several newspapers a day, I learned to be discerning. We studied the individuals and tried to learn what they stood for by listening to all they said and reading all we could about each candidate. My tendency then was to become a conservative, although I still did not recognize the deep differences that existed between the parties. I liked Carter and considered him to be a good man; I also liked the fact that his daughter, Amy, was sent to public school. Burt, however, was very aware of the troubles he put us in with Iran, and pontificated to me, and anyone willing to listen, about it at great length so that I had to defend the president on many occasions, but to no avail.

We were so proud of President Reagan, whom we voted for with great glee. He gave us back our country, and we could actually feel the dignity we all regained as Americans under President Reagan. When we went abroad for our various work-related meetings, it was a palpable presence. We rejoiced when the Berlin Wall fell. When we were invited to go to Hungary for an important meeting after it was freed, it was a whole different experience, having been there the first time when it was still tied to the Soviet Union—which was scary to us all and made me especially uncomfortable, vague feelings of fearful times recurring.

After President Reagan's two terms were up, we voted for George H. W. Bush, and we voted for him a second time, but he lost for his unfortunate expression, "Read my lips," making a promise of not raising taxes he could not fulfill.

GOLDEN AMERICA

I do not want to say much about what followed, except to say that due to the next president's examples, television and the movies followed suit, and the country ran away with it all; filth and violence was all you could see when turning on the TV. The leader had given an example, and people followed his lead. Everything was okay; nothing was left unsaid or undone. The TV, which had entertained us with harmless comedies like Burns and Allen, Lucy and Desi, Sonny and Cher, Cosby, and innocuous mysteries like *Columbo*, *Kojak*, *Perry Mason*, and others gave way to nonsense and filth, such that the TV became obsolete in our house. All we could watch were some reruns of old shows and old movies and the news on CNN. Watching reruns I had to do by myself, for if Burt was near, he would ruin the fun. Whether he had seen the story ten or twenty years ago, his memory would set in, and he could not stop himself from telling me what would happen next.

I worried about the country then as I do now when I see the results. How can young people grow up decent and good when all that could be seen was filth and violence day after day on channel after channel? Even games for little children were a constant presentation of violence. It was all running away from us—most households had parents who were at work during the week, and children could have free rein to watch what was not fit for any human being to see. The moral insensitivity that must result from such fare is so obvious, and yet it continues unstopped. The immorality that programs like *Dr. Ruth* presented to children and young adults alike was abhorrent, as I saw watching her show for four minutes once, by accident. To add to the dissolution of the younger generation, the noise that was called music, instead of being soothing to the soul, turned violent too, rap being at the very top of the list of ugliness.

We were given some relief from turmoil by electing George W. Bush, whom I liked and admired, as I did First Lady Laura for her sweetness and humble manner. But the world had changed in those previous years, and then we suffered the attacks of 9/11. It seemed to come from nowhere as we were unprepared, having left unheeded the signs that had appeared here and there, and Burt and I watched the tragedy unfold in front of our eyes.

Strange destiny had placed us at the Hudson shore, in full view of the Trade Center buildings, which I loved. When Rachel was interviewing for college, the college of her choice invited us for a talk in a hotel next to the Trade Center, and I fell in love with those buildings and that neighborhood I had never explored before. After Rachel started college, we moved to Battery Park City from Whitestone, Queens, which made our travel to work infinitely easier and shorter, the two-hour trips being cut to thirty minutes. This was a boon in itself, but it also put us in a wonderful, luxurious place we really treasured. My extra free time, what with the shorter commute and the fact that Rachel was not waiting at home, could be spent wandering around in the Trade Center buildings, with their fine marble floors and walls and fancy stores, to window shop. There were bookstores and art stores and other specialty stores and cozy coffee shops, and after passing over the little bridge that led to our apartment, we could roam around the Winter Garden in the Financial Center, again all marble and luxury, with sixteen indoor palm trees we affectionately watched grow. We enjoyed concerts there, plays and dances, all for free on some evenings. Every workday, I rejoiced in the walk from the subway to home, passing the two towers, which I had adopted as my own, with their elegant surroundings. On Sundays, we treated ourselves to Au Bon Pain, a favored coffee shop with the most delicious chocolate croissants that melted in your mouth, and little tables allowing Burt to read his Sunday papers, and me to start my puzzle.

Our apartment, which was rather little and very expensive, gave us a view of the Hudson River, my beloved Statue of Liberty, and the Jersey shore. At the end of a year, Burt decided to move us to Jersey City, right across the river, which would afford us the benefit of a larger apartment, not much more of a commute, and the full view of my two buildings, a large part of downtown Manhattan, still the Statue of Liberty, and a better deal for our pocketbook. I was delighted with the view, and he was more comfortable, having more space for his books and papers.

In the beginning of September 2001, strangely enough, I wrote a flowery letter that said, in part,

Dear Rachel,

I sit here, writing to you, overlooking the view I like best—the majestic isle of Manhattan stretched out before me, across the river. The sun is glistening on the shimmery Hudson, boats are passing, making white streaks in the water, helicopters are lazily rumbling back and forth. My Twin Towers stand out and dominate the skyscrapers around them, proud, safe, and awe-inspiring. I am so grateful to the man who had the vision to build the building we live in. He has made it possible that I may have my view, unobstructed, day and night, this place which gives me a wealth, an opulence of sight, an aesthetic whole I can and do luxuriate in, a perfect thing...

View from our apartment before 9/11/01

On the morning of 9/11, a sunny day, I happened to have an appointment with my doctor for a regular checkup, and so Burt decided to go to work later too. Looking out of the window after hearing a loud noise, I started to scream, for one of the Twin Towers was billowing smoke from the top third of its walls. I screamed that a terrible accident must have happened, that an airplane looked to have crashed inside; but a few moments later, we saw in front of us, close enough to make out the markings, another airplane turning a sharp left and aiming right for the other tower. Burt recognized it for what it was—a terrorist attack. He called the police and the FBI, but they told him to calm down, that they would handle it. We both could not stop screaming. We called Rachel and told her what we saw, and later, we called her again, and I screamed into the telephone that the buildings were collapsing, collapsing in front of our eyes. From the TV, we found out about the other two terrorist plots and about the heroic people who lost their lives saving the White House. It was chaos and sadness all over. Normal life had gone forever.

LIFE AFTER 9/11

We were inspired by President Bush and Mayor Giuliani's urgings not to give up and to resume some normalcy as much as possible, so after a week of no more attacks, which we were so worried about, we found a new way to go to work since the PATH trains we usually rode from Jersey to Manhattan were gone. It was a roundabout journey, and we looked over our shoulders more than once each day, noticing the crowds and how vulnerable we all were. Our favorite department technician, Lewis, had lost a sister in the World Trade Center, and we kept hearing of others who had lost loved ones—three thousand innocent victims had lost their lives on American soil, the place that was a haven for everyone who wanted to come and be saved from persecution. It was beyond "getting over," it was beyond comprehension. There was a new world order.

We gladly reelected President Bush, who had shown the enemy from hell that we were not going to take this lying down and had given the order to invade Afghanistan and later Iraq, where these fiends were plotting against us. It was beyond my comprehension that, suddenly, President Bush was vilified in the media for invading Iraq. The premise that no weapons of mass destruction could be found was not proof that there had never been any since most in Congress had agreed that there were, since they had been used against the Iraqi people, and it was easy to hide them or move them to other lands. We got rid of the Butcher of Baghdad, for which President Bush got no thanks, and we were kept safe in our own country by the vigilance that was put in place, for which President Bush again got no thanks. It was infinitely sad that our soldiers were in harm's way, and we paid dearly for these invasions with blood and maiming of our young courageous volunteer army, but we had been attacked on our own soil, and could we just forget about that? We had not started any wars, we had not spoken out against anyone, we had not committed any kind of aggression with words or action before 9/11.

The venom that was written and spoken against the administration became worse as time passed, and with this background, the next election became a fait accompli; it was going to go to the other party.

What followed I would rather not talk about. I became disenchanted and then disillusioned about our wonderful, beautiful country and worried about its future. This country that had given all of us freedom; freedom to move about, freedom to follow our dreams, freedom to work toward what we want to achieve, and freedom not to be harassed by the government. Nowhere else can you be secure to have the right to all that. I and many others like me are certainly proof of that.

We have a Constitution given by the forefathers to We the People, and we have the responsibility to maintain this freedom that many have died for and vote for those who will faithfully keep it as the law of the land. We have the solemn responsibility to check and recheck the candidates we vote for, to do research and look into their backgrounds. Did they have parents who taught them good American values? Do they have friends who are faithful to the Constitution? There is a saying, "Show me your friends, and I'll tell you who you are." Do they realize that there is a division of power in this great land of ours, or do they tend to be dictatorial in their views and actions? Do they know that they work for and are responsible to *We the People*? Do they tell the truth when they make promises as candidates? Are they likely to keep their promises? Does the candidate have an overwhelming and burning desire for power, and does he or she insist on fulfilling this desire no matter what state the country is in, no matter that he or she has done nothing helpful so far for this greatest of countries and has even actually been detrimental to its people?

Voting simply for a party is like voting by covering your eyes tightly with a black cloth and having someone else hold your hand to push the lever in the voting booth!

We cannot take our blessings for granted and leave it to others to do the right thing; it is the duty of each and every one of us to know and read again and again from the Declaration of Independence that *We hold these truths to be self-evident, that all men are created equal, that they are endowed by their Creator with certain unalienable Rights, that among these are Life, Liberty and the Pursuit of Happiness.* And it is our duty to make sure that this is upheld.

Nowhere else does this exist. I know because I lived without it for ten long, painful years, and so do the others who came here, as I did, to be free. But those who are born here, alas, they tend to take it all for granted, and tend to sleep when they should be vigilant to keep this beautiful inheritance they received *for free* from the forefathers and God.

And racism, what is racism? In this day and age, the word really should not exist. When I came to this country, I came from several places that were inhabited purely by Caucasians, and if they did not want to destroy me altogether, they did not want me to stay in their countries. So when I finally got over my stress and trauma and became a citizen here, it was the presence of other races, like the African-Americans, Latinos, Asians, and others, that represented for me, and I am sure for all the others like me, this free land I adored.

I remember (for example) at one of the meetings I attended back in Europe, I gravitated toward an African scientist and talked with him and sat next to him because his presence made me feel more at home.

So racism does not exist in my vocabulary and it should not for others. We are all proud Americans, no matter where we came from.

And the other social issues that are bandied about, why are they even talked about? Is it not part of our Declaration of Independence, and secured by the Constitution and the Bill of Rights, that all men are created equal and have the right to life, liberty, and the pursuit of happiness? Does that not say it all? It should end the discussion, if you are aware of what it truly means. Does that not include freedom of conduct as long as no one is hurt by it, freedom of religion (or nonreligion) without willfully imposing it on others, freedom of speech, and freedom to protect oneself and be protected?

THE CHOSEN PEOPLE

It is said that we Jews are the chosen people. I have often wondered what that meant. We are certainly not chosen because we are the smartest people. We definitely are not, although this idea has created jealousy, yet it is totally unsubstantiated and has given us great grief. We are certainly not chosen because we are privileged people because that too is not true. We are certainly not chosen because we are in any way better than other people because we decidedly are not. I have come to the conclusion that we are chosen for only one thing and that is to follow our religion as much as we possibly can, not because it is the one true religion, but because it is what we were ordered and promised to do almost six thousand years ago. We were chosen to follow the Commandments as much as we possibly can, and the summary of these are "Do not do unto others what you would not have them do unto you" and "Be as good and gentle a person as you can possibly be." We were chosen to do just that and by it set an example to the world for goodness and kindness and fairness and ethics—in other words, to follow and share the following from the Ten Commandments:

> Don't swear falsely.
> Keep the Sabbath.
> Honor your parents.
> Don't murder.
> Don't commit adultery.
> Don't steal.
> Don't bear false witness.
> Don't covet what others have.

But then, to my mind, we Americans, we are all the *chosen people* because we derive a gift from our Judeo-Christian faith, the pilgrims and our wise and courageous forefathers, who gave us that unique experiment: the US Constitution.

And now I am worried about my beloved golden America because many seem to have forgotten all that is good in this land (many of my sisters and brothers have even forgotten what it means to be Jewish and many of my Christian friends are forgetting their beautiful ethical faith). They all follow ideas that are un-American and falsehoods that will lead us to enslavement. We are no longer that "Shining City on the Hill" nor do we seem to act in accordance to that precious gift that made us so exceptional: the US Constitution.

I would like to shout out to the citizens and citizens-to-be, one and all, and especially to the young people growing up: be careful and see the facts; wake up to the light. We are drowning in a mess of false mandates, bad laws, useless regulations, and ways of doing things that are dragging us down and are making us captive. It is up to us, each and every one of us, to return to the right path and retain the greatest of treasures: *freedom for all.*

ABOUT THE AUTHOR

Bella Altura was born in a small town in Germany, a Jewish girl in a proper Jewish home. She had a happy childhood until the Nazis ransacked her home in the night of November 9, 1938. An existence of anxiety followed, yet her family was able to elude the concentration camps by wandering through Belgium and France, ending up in Switzerland, where her parents were placed in internment camps and she in various foster homes. Enduring a decade of fear, the family immigrated to America. Soon after, her mother died and Bella attended school, while caring for her father's home. After college, she became ill and had to be hospitalized, the stress, having caught up with her. She recovered with some help, was able to get a position in a biochemistry lab and later attended graduate school at night and obtained a master's and PhD degree in physiology. She married, had a daughter, and worked in her husband's lab, proceeding from Research Associate to Research Professor. She is author and co-author of many scientific papers and shares numerous international honors.

Printed in the USA
CPSIA information can be obtained
at www.ICGtesting.com
LVHW041119181024
794097LV00002B/476